Family Bible QUIZ BOOK

Vic Parker

Miles Kelly

First published in 2013 by Miles Kelly Publishing Ltd
Harding's Barn, Bardfield End Green, Thaxted, Essex, CM6 3PX, UK

2 4 6 8 10 9 7 5 3 1

Publishing Director Belinda Gallagher
Creative Director Jo Cowan
Editorial Director Rosie McGuire
Senior Editor Carly Blake
Assistant Editor Amy Johnson
Designer Rob Hale
Consultant Janet Dyson
Production Manager Elizabeth Collins
Reprographics Stephan Davis, Jennifer Hunt, Thom Allaway

ISBN 978-1-78209-099-1

Printed in China

British Library Cataloguing-in-Publication Data
A catalogue record for this book is available from the British Library

ACKNOWLEDGEMENTS
The publishers would like to thank Jan Lewis for the artwork she contributed to this book.
All other artwork from the Miles Kelly Artwork Bank.

The publishers would like to thank the following sources for the use of their photographs:
Fotolia.com (background, used throughout) Alexey Khromushin
Shutterstock.com Quiz 6 (dove) basel101658, (frog) Zara's Gallery, (bat) Nikola m,
(lion) abracadabra, (calf) ananas; Quiz 23 (camel) Aleksandr Sulga, (fox) lantapix, (ant) Roman Sotola,
(peacock) John David Bigl III, (lamb) lantapix; Quiz 56 (donkey) lantapix, (pig) oorka,
(cockerel) Klaus Kaulitzki, (fish) Adam Tinney, (wolf) abracadabra; Quiz 73 (locust) Slobodan Djajic,
(sparrow) basel101658, (whale) Viktorya170377, (scorpion) lantapix, (dragon) Elena Kazanskaya

Every effort has been made to acknowledge the source and copyright holder of each picture.
Miles Kelly Publishing apologizes for any unintentional errors or omissions.

Made with paper from a sustainable forest

www.mileskelly.net   info@mileskelly.net

Contents

How to Use

There are two sections in this book — Old Testament and New Testament. Each section contains 50 quizzes. You can do the quizzes on your own, against a partner or in teams.

The quizzes are numbered from one to 100.

Both sections have three levels: Easy, Medium and Hard. These colour-coded tabs tell you which level you are in.

Answers for each quiz are given at the bottom of the page. Bible references are provided where necessary. All references given are from the Revised Standard Version of the Bible.

Picture clues help you answer certain questions.

At the end of each section is a well-known Bible story, followed by a quiz. The answers can be found within the story.

Scoresheets

You can use the scoresheets to keep a record of your scores. Just go to the kids' area of www.mileskelly.net and print out copies for each player or team.

At the end of each level, add up your scores to get your total.

Fill in your score for each quiz.

When you have completed a section, add up your scores for each level to work out your Old or New Testament score. If you have finished both sections, you can then fill in your total for the whole book.

Old Testament

1 How many days did God take to create the world?

2 What did God create to look just like him?

3 Which bone did God take from Adam to create the first woman?

4 What was the name of the first woman?

5 Which animal with a woolly coat and horns did Abraham sacrifice on a mountainside, instead of his son?

6 What else did God create, along with the moon and the stars?

7 Which animal did the pharaoh see in a dream, which he asked Joseph to explain?

8 Which colour is also the name of the sea that parted so the Israelites could cross it?

9 What type of boat did Noah build?

10 What place was Daniel thrown into that was full of lions?

Who Am I?

Read the clues and look at the pictures for each person to work out who they are.

 1 I was the first man. God made me out of some dust. He put me in charge of all his creatures.

 2 I made an enormous boat. I was 950 years old when I died. My three sons were called Shem, Ham and Japheth.

3 I had a wife called Sarah. God led me to a place known as the Promised Land. I was 86 years old when my first child was born.

4 Jacob was my father. He gave me a beautiful, expensive coat. My brothers were very jealous of me.

 5 I was born in Egypt. I was hidden in a basket and put into a river. When I grew up, I led the Israelites out of Egypt.

EASY

3

True or False?

Read these statements and decide
whether they are true or false.

1 Moses was in a forest when God spoke to him from a burning bush.

2 Daniel stayed in the lions' den for one week.

3 The tree from which Adam and Eve ate fruit was called the Tree of Knowledge of Good and Evil.

4 God once destroyed two cities because the people who lived there were wicked.

5 Joseph gave the pharaoh advice about how to protect Egypt from the famine, but the pharaoh ignored it.

6 Moses broke the first stone tablets that God gave him on which the Ten Commandments were written.

7 Copies of the stone tablets were kept in a chest called the Ark of the Covenant.

8 When Samuel heard God calling him in the night, he thought it was the priest he lived with, called Eli.

9 King Solomon had one wife.

10 In the wilderness, the Israelites built a big, special tent called the Tabernacle in which to worship God.

For each question, the first letter
of the answer is given as a clue.

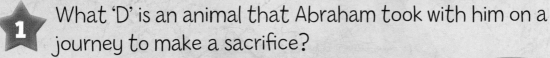

1 What 'D' is an animal that Abraham took with him on a journey to make a sacrifice?

2 What 'T' is a place of prayer that King Solomon built?

3 What 'S' did Moses usually carry in his hand?

QUESTION 1

4 What 'G' was the name of the giant killed by the shepherd boy, David?

5 What 'K' was Nebuchadnezzar, the man who ordered Shadrach, Meshach and Abednego into a furnace?

6 What 'R' did God put in the sky after flooding the world?

7 What 'W' did the Israelites ask Moses for in the desert when they were thirsty?

8 What 'A' appeared in the furnace with Shadrach, Meshach and Abednego?

QUESTION 8

9 What 'T' did priests blow to bring the walls of Jericho tumbling down?

10 What 'C' did God make for Adam and Eve when they became ashamed of being naked?

ANSWERS: 1. Donkey (Genesis 22:3–6) **2.** Temple (1 Kings 6, 7, 8) **3.** Staff (Exodus 17:1–3) **4.** Goliath (1 Samuel 17:4) **5.** King (Daniel 1:1) **6.** Rainbow (Genesis 9:13) **7.** Water (Exodus 17:1–3) **8.** Angel (Daniel 3:25) **9.** Trumpets (Joshua 6:1–6) **10.** Clothes (Genesis 3:21)

Multiple Choice

Select the correct answer from
the three choices given.

1 Which creature tempted Eve to commit a sin?
a a serpent **b** a spider **c** a scorpion

2 What did Adam and Eve commit a sin by eating?
a a nut **b** a vegetable **c** a piece of fruit

3 What type of weather did God destroy the world with?
a hail **b** rain **c** snow

4 What were Shadrach, Meshach and Abednego put into?
a a fiery furnace **b** a deep, dark pit **c** a tiny prison cell

5 What was the name of the boy who killed a giant?
a Daniel **b** Darius **c** David

6 What was King Solomon famous for being?
a very wise **b** very foolish **c** very brave

7 What swallowed up Jonah?
a a big dinosaur **b** a big fish **c** a big hole

8 How did the prophet Elijah travel up to Heaven?
a a chariot of fire **b** a puff of smoke **c** winged sandals

9 Joseph could tell the meaning of what?
a tea leaves **b** dreams **c** doodles

10 What was Samson's special power?
a super-sight **b** super-speed **c** super-strength

What Am I?

Read the clues and look at the picture hints to help you identify these animals.

1 I have wings. Noah sent me out of the ark twice to see if there was land. The second time, I returned with an olive leaf.

2 I jump and swim. I was one of nine plagues that God sent upon Egypt. I came onto land during the plague.

3 I fly at night. God told Moses that I should not be eaten. I was written about in the Book of Leviticus.

4 I am large and fierce. Daniel was put into my den as punishment for praying to God. I did not eat him.

5 I am a baby animal. Moses' brother made a gold statue of me. God was angry when the Israelites worshipped the statue.

ANSWERS 1. Dove (Genesis 8:8–11) **2.** Frog (Exodus 9:6) **3.** Bat (Leviticus 11:9) **4.** Lion (Daniel 6) **5.** Calf (Exodus 32)

How Many?

All of these questions can be
answered with a number.

1 How many ravens did Noah send out of the ark to look for land?

2 How many days did Jonah spend inside the big fish?

3 How many commandments did God give to Moses?

4 How many stone tablets were the commandments written on in total?

5 How many of Daniel's friends were placed in a furnace?

6 How many of each creature did Noah take into the ark?

7 How many brothers did Joseph have?

8 How many years did the Israelites wander before entering the Promised Land?

9 How many days did the Israelite army march around Jericho before the walls came tumbling down?

10 How many plagues did God send upon Egypt?

All About Moses

Test how much you know
about this important leader.

1. Baby Moses was hidden in a basket made of what — reeds or straw?

2. The basket was placed in which river — the river Jordan or the river Nile?

3. Who found Moses — the pharaoh's daughter or the pharaoh's wife?

4. Who named Moses — his mother or the person who found him at the river?

5. What was the name of Moses' brother — Aaron or Aalan?

6. What was Moses' wife's name — Zipporah or Zuleika?

7. What did Moses do to an Egyptian man he saw beating an Israelite — told him to stop or killed him?

8. How old was Moses when he went to the pharaoh to demand the release of the Israelites — 18 or 80?

9. How old was Moses when he died — 120 or 125 years old?

10. Where did Moses die — Mount Sinai or Mount Nebo?

Moses

ANSWERS: 1. Reeds (Exodus 2:3) 2. The river Nile (Exodus 2:1–10) 3. The pharaoh's daughter (Exodus 2:1–10) 4. The person who found him (Exodus 2:10) 5. Aaron (Exodus 3:14) 6. Zipporah (Exodus 18:2) 7. He killed him (Exodus 2:12) 8. 80 (Exodus 7:7) 9. 120 years old (Deuteronomy 34:7) 10. Mount Nebo (Deuteronomy 34:1)

Anagram Antics

Read the clues and unscramble the letters to work out the answers.

 1 **need** The name of the garden God created for Adam and Eve to live in.

 2 **inac** Adam and Eve's first son.

 3 **leab** Adam and Eve's second son.

 4 **dniw** God sent this to scorch Jonah when he was in the desert.

 5 **hubs** Moses saw this growing in the desert and it looked like it was on fire.

 6 **hurt** This girl lived with her mother-in-law to look after her, and both were very poor.

 7 **norc** The pharaoh saw two stalks of this – one healthy and one shrivelled – in a dream.

 8 **gtoa** Jacob wore the skin of this animal to disguise himself from his father.

 9 **gnik** Another word for 'pharaoh'.

 10 **yabb** The pharaoh's daughter found this at the edge of the river Nile.

Place Puzzler

These questions are all
about important places.

1 What did Noah's ark come to rest upon after the flood – a mountain top or a valley floor?

2 Which country did God promise to give to Abraham – Canada or Canaan?

3 Where did Adam and Eve first live – in a cave or in a garden?

4 Where were the Israelites held as slaves for 400 years – Egypt or Ethiopia?

QUESTION 4

5 Where did Gideon and his neighbours hide from a desert tribe – in the hills or in the marshlands?

6 What did the Israelites cross to reach the Promised Land – the river Jordan or the river Amazon?

7 Where did the Israelites wander for many years – in the jungle or in the desert?

8 Where did a big fish spit Jonah out – at sea or onto dry land?

QUESTION 8

9 Where did Solomon construct amazing buildings – Jericho or Jerusalem?

10 Where did Esther become a princess – Peru or Persia?

ANSWERS 1. A mountain top (Genesis 8:4) 2. Canaan (Genesis 12:5) 3. In a garden (Genesis 2:8) 4. Egypt 5. In the hills (Judges 6:1–3) 6. The river Jordan (Joshua 3) 7. A desert (Exodus 15, 16, 17) 8. Onto dry land (Jonah 2:10) 9. Jerusalem (1 Kings 5, 6, 7) 10. Persia (Esther 1:3)

1 What was the profession of the people who threw Jonah overboard?

2 God turned Lot's wife into a pillar of what?

3 What is the word for the people that Moses sent secretly into the Promised Land?

4 What was David's job when he was a young boy?

5 What stopped Daniel escaping from the lions' den?

6 Who was the youngest of Jacob's sons?

7 What was the name of Sarah's servant?

8 Why were Shadrach, Meshach and Abednego placed in a fiery furnace?

9 What animals did Aaron and the pharaoh's magicians turn their staffs into?

10 Who was Jacob's favourite son?

Test how much you know about the terrible punishments God sent upon Egypt.

1 What did God send in the sixth plague – baldness or boils?

2 In the fourth plague, what arrived in swarms – bees or flies?

3 What did God send in the seventh plague – hail or a hurricane?

4 In the ninth plague, God sent darkness for how many days – three or 13?

5 What died in the fifth plague – the Egyptians' animals or their crops?

6 In the first plague, what did the water of the river Nile turn into – wine or blood?

7 In the third plague, what turned into gnats – dust or leaves?

8 What type of insect did God send in the eighth plague – locusts or ants?

9 What covered the land in the second plague – frogs or fish?

10 Which festival celebrates how the Jews were saved from the tenth plague – Hanukkah or Passover?

QUESTION 1

QUESTION 8

ANSWERS 1. Boils (Exodus 9:8–12) 2. Flies (Exodus 8:20–32) 3. Hail (Exodus 9:13–26) 4. Three (Exodus 10:23) 5. The Egyptians' animals (Exodus 9:1–7) 6. Blood (Exodus 7:20) 7. Dust (Exodus 8:17) 8. Locusts (Exodus 10:4–20) 9. Frogs (Exodus 8:8–15) 10. Passover (Exodus 12:14–27)

EASY

13

Missing Link

Complete each statement using one
of the words from the boxes below.

1 Abraham was very rich in cattle, silver and _ _ _ _ .

2 Joseph dreamed of being bowed to by the sun, moon and eleven _ _ _ _ _ .

3 Three of the Ten Commandments were not to lie, not to steal and to use God's name with _ _ _ _ _ _ _ .

4 Three Old Testament prophets were Elijah, Elisha and _ _ _ _ _ .

5 Noah's sons were Shem, Ham and _ _ _ _ _ _ _ .

stars

Japheth

Jonah

gold

respect

Family Connections

Match these family members with their relationship to each other.

 1 Adam and Eve

 2 Jacob and Esau

 3 Abraham and Lot

 4 Moses and Miriam

 5 Esther and Mordecai

QUESTION 2

QUESTION 4

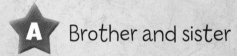 **A** Brother and sister

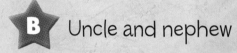 **B** Uncle and nephew

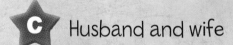 **C** Husband and wife

 **D** Cousins

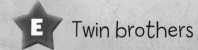 **E** Twin brothers

EASY

15 Read and Remember

Read this short story and try to
remember as much as you can.

The Creation
(Genesis 1 and 2)

In the beginning, God lived in darkness. There was nothing except water rushing over a shapeless mass of land.

Then God said, "Let there be light!" and there was. God liked the light. After a while, he called back the darkness. He called this day and night.

God called the light back to create the second day. He looked at the waters below and at the nothingness above. God wanted a roof to curve over the water, so he ordered half of the water up, to swirl above. God called it the sky.

On the third day, God ordered some of the water to move aside, so land could show through. This worked well and God named the bits of water and the areas of land, sea and earth. 'The earth looks bare,' God thought, and suddenly grass and flowers and trees began to blossom everywhere.

On day four, God decorated the sky. He

placed in it the sun, moon and millions of stars. He set them moving in careful patterns that would mark the passing of the days, seasons and years.

On the fifth day, God decided he wanted things to live in his new world. He began creating all sorts of creatures to live in the sea. Then he did the same for the sky. On the sixth day, he created creatures to live on the earth. Finally, God was happy with everything he had created. But who was going to look after it all?

God bent down and scooped up some dust. He squashed it into a figure that looked like himself. He breathed into its nostrils, and it came to life. It was the first man, Adam. God didn't want Adam to be lonely, so he modelled another figure from one of Adam's ribs – the first woman, Eve.

On the seventh day, God rested and admired his creation. He ordered that, from then on, every seventh day should be a special holy day of rest, in memory of when he completed his work.

Now, test your memory on what you have read by answering these questions.

1 What was the first thing that God created?

2 What did God create on the second day?

3 Why did God create the sun, moon and stars?

4 What did God make first – creatures for the sky or creatures for the sea?

5 On what day did God make creatures for the land?

6 What did God create Adam from?

7 How did God bring Adam to life?

8 Which of Adam's bones did God make Eve from?

9 God ordered that every seventh day should be a holy day of what?

10 How many days did God take to create the world, not including the day he rested?

ANSWERS 1. Light 2. The sky 3. To mark the passing of days, seasons and years 4. Creatures for the sea 5. The sixth day 6. Dust 7. God breathed into Adam's nostrils 8. His rib 9. Rest 10. Six

16 True or False?

Read these statements and decide whether they are true or false.

1 Moses led the Israelites into the Promised Land.

2 The door of the ark was closed by Noah.

3 Adam and Eve made clothes for themselves out of palm leaves.

4 The child that the prophet Elisha brought back to life was a boy.

5 There were once people so proud of themselves that they tried to build a tower that reached up to Heaven.

6 Joseph's brothers sold him to slave traders.

7 Isaac's son, Esau, was older than his twin, Jacob.

8 The prophet Elisha was the teacher of the prophet Elijah.

9 God gave instructions for making the Ark of the Covenant to Noah.

10 The boat that Jonah boarded was headed for Tarshish.

ANSWERS 1. False — it was Joshua (Joshua 1) 2. False — it was closed by God (Genesis 7:16) 3. False — fig leaves (Genesis 3:7) 4. True (2 Kings 4:32–37) 5. True (Genesis 11:1–9) 6. True (Genesis 37:28) 7. True (Genesis 25:25–26) 8. False — the prophet Elijah taught the prophet Elisha (1 Kings 19:19–21) 9. False — God gave instructions to Moses (Exodus 25:1–22) 10. True (Jonah 1:3)

Who Am I?

Read the clues and look at the pictures for each person to work out who they are.

1 I was a prophet. I disobeyed God. A big fish swallowed me and I spent three days and nights inside it.

2 I grew up in a temple as a servant to Eli. One night, God called me. I became a prophet and a ruler of Israel.

3 I was a warrior. I led the Israelites into the Promised Land. I commanded my army to march around Jericho for seven days.

4 I was very strong. I killed a lion with my bare hands. I had long hair, but when it was cut off, I lost my strength.

5 I lived in Persia and had a cousin called Mordecai. I married King Xerxes. I stopped the king from killing the Jews.

18

How Many?

All of these questions can be
answered with a number.

1. How many days and nights did God send rain to flood the earth?

2. How many decks did Noah's ark have?

3. How many people were on the ark?

4. How many years of famine did Joseph warn the pharaoh were coming?

5. How many sons did Jesse, the father of David the shepherd boy, have?

6. How many stones did David put in his shepherd's bag when he set out to fight Goliath?

7. How many times did the Israelites march round Jericho on the seventh day?

8. How many cubits tall (plus a span) was Goliath?

9. How many psalms are contained in the Book of Psalms?

10. How many Philistines did Samson say he had killed with the jaw bone of a donkey?

ANSWERS: 1. 40 days and nights (Genesis 7:4) **2.** Three (Genesis 6:16) **3.** Eight (Genesis 8:13) **4.** Seven (Genesis 41:27) **5.** Eight (1 Samuel 17:12) **6.** Five (1 Samuel 17:40) **7.** Seven (Joshua 6:15) **8.** Six cubits and a span (1 Samuel 17:4) **9.** 150 **10.** 1000 (Judges 15:16)

Initial Inquiry

For each question, the first letter of the answer is given as a clue.

1 Which person beginning with 'B' did Jacob not send to Egypt to fetch grain during the famine?

2 Which 'J' asked God to make the sun stand still?

3 Which 'W' was sent by God to scorch Jonah in the desert?

4 Which 'A' was the mountain range on which Noah's ark came to rest?

5 What 'M' is the name of the oldest person in the Bible, who died at the age of 969 years?

6 What 'G' was a man whom God told to lead the Israelites against the Midianites?

7 What 'S' is the mount on which Moses received the Ten Commandments?

8 What 'H' was the secret of Samson's great strength?

9 What 'J' was the wicked wife of King Ahab?

10 What 'B' did two women argue over, before King Solomon settled their quarrel?

QUESTION 1

QUESTION 6

Anagram Antics

Read the clues and unscramble the letters to work out the answers.

 1   arbaahm   A man ordered by God to sacrifice his son.

 2   yohen   A type of food that Samson found inside the body of a dead lion.

 3   metelp   The building where the high priest Eli lived with his servant.

 4   rueebn   The brother who intended to rescue Joseph after his other brothers had attacked him.

 5   marimi   Moses' sister.

 6   kao   Gideon saw an angel sitting under this type of tree while he was threshing wheat.

 7   oskeynd   Saul lost three of these animals, just before he was anointed king.

8   dinbl   This word describes Samson after the Philistines took out his eyes.

9   kar fo teh vocentan   This was built to keep the Ten Commandments in.

 10   clya   God once showed the prophet Jeremiah a potter modelling this on his wheel.

Signs and Symbols

Answer these questions about significant signs and symbols.

21

1 What did the dove bring back to the ark as a sign that the flood had gone?

2 What was the rainbow a sign of?

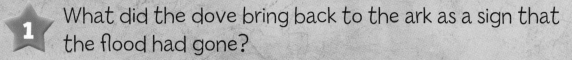

QUESTION 1

3 What tool did Elisha make float on water, as a sign that he was a holy man?

4 What animal's skin did Gideon place on the ground, asking God to give him a sign?

5 As the Israelites marched around Jericho, what sound was used as a sign for them to start shouting?

6 What was the first sign God told Moses to show the Israelites, as proof that God had sent him?

7 What was the second sign God told Moses to show the Israelites?

QUESTION 6

8 What was the third sign God told Moses to show the Israelites?

9 What did God tell the Israelites to put on their doorposts to mark out their houses?

10 What piece of jewellery did the pharaoh give to Joseph when he made him ruler of Egypt?

1 What was the name of Jacob's mother?

 2 Moses was hidden among which type of plant at the edge of the river Nile?

 3 Which Old Testament book begins with an 'R'?

 4 In which city did Rahab hide two Israelite spies?

 5 Who was the father of Rachel and Leah?

6 Which river did Joshua lead the Israelite army across to enter the Promised Land?

 7 Which type of bird fed the prophet Elijah while he was in the wilderness?

 8 How did Moses produce water in the wilderness?

 9 What did King David give to an Egyptian who had not eaten for three days?

 10 How did God punish Cain for killing his brother?

What Am I?

Read the clues and look at the picture hints to help you identify these animals.

 1 I live in the desert. Jacob's wives and sons rode on me to go to Canaan. I also carried their possessions.

 **2** I have a bushy tail. Samson once attached a torch to my tail and let me go. I set fire to the Philistines' fields.

 3 I am a type of insect. I am mentioned in the Book of Proverbs. It says that people should follow my example and be hard-working.

 **4** I have a beautiful tail. King Solomon brought me into Israel. I came on a ship from a place called Tarshish.

 5 People keep me in flocks. Nathan told King David a story about me. In the story, I was stolen by a rich man.

24 Multiple Choice

Select the correct answer from
the three choices given.

1 What was Jacob's twin brother's name?
a Esau **b** Ezra **c** Ezekiel

2 Which of these did God create first?
a the sky **b** the land **c** the stars

3 Which of these did the pharaoh give to Joseph?
a silver sandals **b** the pharaoh's own ring **c** a palace

4 Which of these cities was ruled by King Hiram?
a Beirut **b** Tripoli **c** Tyre

5 Which of these is a book of the Old Testament?
a Genesis **b** Hebrews **c** Matthew

6 What did Jacob dream of one night in the desert?
a a ladder to Heaven **b** a road to the sea **c** stairs to Hell

7 What does one of the Commandments say not to do?
a argue **b** mock **c** lie

8 Joseph's coat was dipped in the blood of which animal?
a a sheep **b** a goat **c** a camel

9 Which of these was not a plague on Egypt?
a blood **b** darkness **c** sickness

10 Who was the stranger that Jacob wrestled with?
a the devil **b** God **c** Abraham

Test how much you know
about Jacob's favourite son.

Joseph

1. Who was Joseph's mother — Rachel or Rebecca?

2. Joseph was which of Jacob's twelve sons — the tenth or the eleventh?

3. How old was Joseph when Jacob had a special coat made for him — 17 or 18?

4. Joseph's brothers threw him into what — a dried-up well or an old mine tunnel?

5. How many shekels of silver did Joseph's brothers sell him for — 20 or 30?

6. What was the name of the captain that Joseph worked for — Pilate or Potiphar?

7. How old was Joseph when the pharaoh put him in charge of the country — 30 or 33?

8. Who was Joseph's favourite brother — Benjamin or Simeon?

9. What did Joseph order to be put into his favourite brother's grain sack — a silver plate or a silver cup?

10. Who was Joseph's wife — Asenath or Abigail?

ANSWERS: 1. Rachel (Genesis 35:24) **2.** The eleventh (Genesis 30:23–24) **3.** 17 years old (Genesis 37:2) **4.** A dried-up well (Genesis 37:20–24) **5.** 20 (Genesis 37:28) **6.** Potiphar (Genesis 37:36) **7.** 30 years old (Genesis 41:46) **8.** Benjamin (Genesis 43:30–34) **9.** A silver cup (Genesis 44:2) **10.** Asenath (Genesis 46:20)

26 Check Your Spelling

Select the correct spelling of
these Old Testament words.

1 A type of ancient coin:
a shekal **b** sheckel **c** shekel

2 A Babylonian king:
a Nebucadnezzar **b** Nebuchadnezzar **c** Nebuchaddnezar

3 A word for 'king':
a pharaoh **b** pharoah **c** pharoh

4 Moses' brother:
a Airon **b** Aaron **c** Aeron

5 The kingdom of the Promised Land:
a Israel **b** Isreal **c** Israil

6 These people were the enemies of the Israelites:
a Philistines **b** Phillistines **c** Phyllistines

7 Joseph became a ruler of this country:
a Eygpt **b** Eegypt **c** Egypt

8 One of 150 poems in a book of the Old Testament:
a psarm **b** psalm **c** palsm

9 A large tent that the Israelites made in which to worship:
a tabernacal **b** tabarnacle **c** tabernacle

10 The grandfather of Noah:
a Methuselah **b** Methusalah **c** Methusela

Into the Wilderness

27

Test how much you know about the Israelites'
escape from Egypt and journey through the desert.

1 What disguised God as he led the Israelites through the desert by day — a pillar of cloud or a pillar of fire?

2 For how many years were the Israelites enslaved in Egypt — 430 or 530?

3 What did Moses use to part the waves of the Red Sea — his hand or his foot?

4 How many men did Moses send to spy on Canaan — 12 or 15?

5 What did God send to bite the Israelites because they were sinful — ants or serpents?

6 After the Israelites had escaped, how did Miriam lead the celebrations — with singing or with a feast?

7 Where did the Israelites wander — the Sahara desert or the Sinai desert?

8 God sent the Israelites a type of bread called manna — was it sweet or salty?

9 God did not send manna on which day of the week — the first or seventh?

10 What did Moses cover his face with after speaking to God — a veil or a mask?

QUESTION 1

QUESTION 8

ANSWERS 1. A pillar of cloud (Exodus 13:21) 2. 430 (Exodus 12:40–41) 3. His hand (Exodus 14:21) 4. 12 (Numbers 13:1–16) 5. Serpents (Exodus 21:6) 6. With singing (Exodus 15:20) 7. The Sinai desert (Exodus 19:1) 8. Sweet — like honey (Exodus 16:32) 9. The seventh day of the week — the Sabbath (Exodus 16:26) 10. A veil (Exodus 34:35).

Timeline Teaser

Test yourself on the order of
Old Testament events.

 1 Who was born first — Abraham or Noah?

 2 What did Joseph dream first — the sun, moon and stars bowing to him, or his brothers' wheat bowing to his?

 3 Who was born first — Ishmael or Isaac?

 4 What happened first — the Israelites' escape from Egypt or the fall of Jericho?

 5 Which was built first — the Ark of the Covenant or the golden calf?

 6 Who ruled Israel first — kings or judges?

 7 Whose victory came first — Gideon's over the Midianites, or David's over Goliath?

 8 What happened first — King Solomon built the Temple, or the Queen of Sheba visited Jerusalem?

 9 What happened first — Daniel was thrown into a pit of lions, or his friends were cast into a fiery furnace?

 10 Which kingdom of the Promised Land was conquered by invaders first — Israel or Judah?

Perfect Partners

Find the missing name in these well-known pairs.

1 Adam and _ _ _

2 Cain and _ _ _ _

3 Jacob and _ _ _ _

4 David and _ _ _ _ _ _ _

5 King Xerxes and _ _ _ _ _ _

QUESTION 2

6 Samson and _ _ _ _ _ _ _

QUESTION 6

7 Naomi and _ _ _ _

8 Abraham and _ _ _ _ _

9 Elkanah and _ _ _ _ _ _

10 Moses and _ _ _ _ _

30 Books Bamboozler

Decide whether each of these statements about the books of the Old Testament is true or false.

 1 There are 40 books in the Old Testament.

 2 Hebrews is not an Old Testament book.

 3 The Book of Psalms is a book of wise sayings.

 4 The Book of Proverbs is a book of poetry and songs.

 5 God is not mentioned in the Book of Esther.

 6 Psalms is the shortest book in the Old Testament.

 7 There is an Old Testament book called Numbers.

 8 Much of the Book of Psalms was written by King David.

 9 Much of the Book of Proverbs was written by King Solomon.

 10 The Ten Commandments are found in the Book of Genesis.

Read and Remember

Read this short story and try to
remember as much as you can.

31

MEDIUM

Noah's Ark
(Genesis 6, 7, 8, 9:1–17)

Adam and Eve had many children, grandchildren and great-grandchildren. As time passed, there came to be many thousands of people living all over the world. But gradually, everyone forgot about God and began behaving very badly.

God saw that his beautiful creation was filled with evil. There was so much wickedness that God felt sorry he had made the world at all. He decided to destroy everything and start again. But one man had remembered God and tried to live a good life — an honest, hard-working farmer called Noah. So God decided to save him, along with his wife and three sons, Shem, Ham and Japheth, and their wives.

God spoke to Noah and explained, "There is evil all around you, so I am going to make an end to all living creatures — but I promise that you and your family will be safe, just do as I tell you. I want you to make an enormous, covered boat — an ark. Make it of the best wood and build it 300 cubits long, 50 cubits wide,

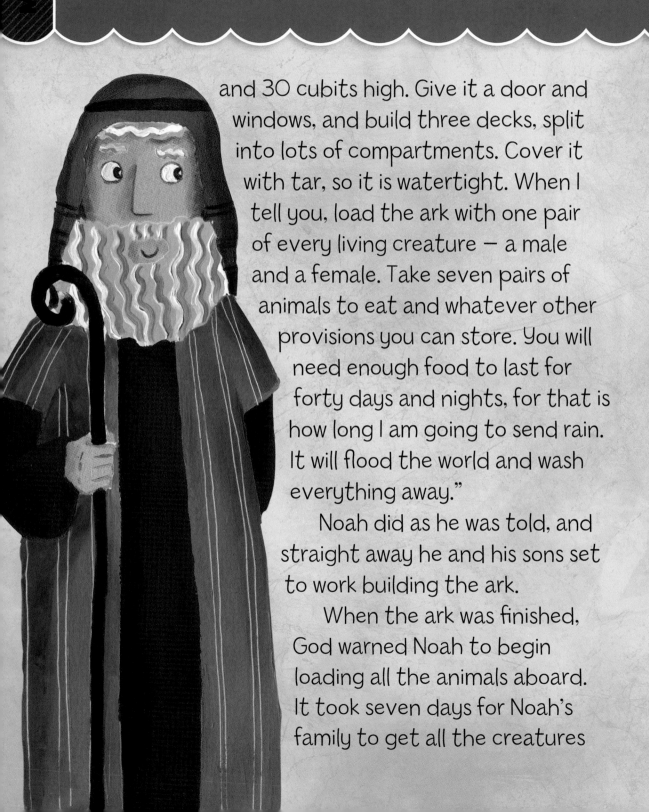

and 30 cubits high. Give it a door and windows, and build three decks, split into lots of compartments. Cover it with tar, so it is watertight. When I tell you, load the ark with one pair of every living creature — a male and a female. Take seven pairs of animals to eat and whatever other provisions you can store. You will need enough food to last for forty days and nights, for that is how long I am going to send rain. It will flood the world and wash everything away."

Noah did as he was told, and straight away he and his sons set to work building the ark.

When the ark was finished, God warned Noah to begin loading all the animals aboard. It took seven days for Noah's family to get all the creatures on. The next day Noah's family went inside the ark, and God closed the door. This happened on the seventeenth day of the second month, when Noah was 600 years old.

Immediately, the skies darkened with thunder clouds and it began to pour with rain. It was as if the skies had cracked open and waterfalls plunged down on the earth. The water quickly rose as high as the mountains, drowning everything. It rained for forty days and nights, just as God had said. But the ark was lifted up and floated safely on the swirling waters.

Then at last, the rain stopped. Noah peered out of a window and saw water in all directions.

In the days that followed, the sun slowly began to dry up the water. God sent a wind to speed things along. Finally, with a loud scrape and shudder, the bottom of the ark came to rest on Mount Ararat.

Noah waited a few days, then sent a raven out – but all it found was water. Noah waited a week, then sent out a dove – but again it returned with no sign of land. After another week, he sent out the dove again and it came back with an olive branch from a tree.

Noah waited one week more and sent out the dove again. It did not return.

Then Noah opened the door of the ark — it was surrounded by dry land. He heard God saying, "Noah, it is time for you and your family to go out into the world with the animals and begin again." So that's what Noah did, along with his family.

When they left the ark, the first thing Noah did was build an altar and give thanks to God for saving them. God blessed the faithful man and his family. He put a rainbow in the sky, as a sign of his promise never again to flood the world and destroy everything.

Now, test your memory on what you have read by answering these questions.

 **1** Why did God save Noah and his family?

 2 How many sons did Noah have?

 3 How many cubits long was the ark?

 4 How many cubits wide was the ark?

 5 How many cubits high was the ark?

 6 How many pairs of animals did God tell Noah to take for eating?

 7 How long did it take to load all the animals onto the ark?

 8 On what date did Noah send the flood?

 9 What type of branch did the dove bring back to the ark?

 10 What was the first thing Noah did after leaving the ark?

ANSWERS: 1. Noah had remembered God and tried to live a good life. 2. Three 3. 300 cubits long 4. 50 cubits wide 5. 30 cubits high 6. Seven 7. Seven days 8. The seventeenth day of the second month 9. An olive branch. 10. He built an altar and gave thanks to God

32

Famous Firsts

Answer these questions about firsts in the Old Testament.

1 What is the first book of the Old Testament?

2 What are the first three words of the Old Testament?

3 What was the name of Abraham's first son?

4 Which creature was first to leave the ark?

5 Who were the first people to commit a sin?

6 What was the first of the ten plagues of Egypt?

7 Which son of Adam and Eve was the first murderer?

8 Moses' brother, Aaron, was Israel's first what?

9 What is the first of the Ten Commandments?

10 Othniel was Israel's first what — judge or king?

Who Am I?

Read the clues and look at the pictures for each person to work out who they are.

1 I was an important prophet. I lived during the reign of the evil King Ahab. God took me up to Heaven in a chariot of fire.

2 I lived in Egypt. I was Moses' older sister. I watched over him when he was placed in the river Nile as a baby.

3 I was a Jew in exile in Babylon. My friends were Meshach and Abednego. We were put into a furnace, but God kept us safe.

4 I could tell the meaning of dreams. I refused to stop praying to God. I was thrown to lions, but God protected me.

5 I was king of the Medes and Persians. I seized the throne of Babylon. I was tricked into throwing my advisor into a pit of lions.

34 True or False?

Read these statements and decide whether they are true or false.

 1 Naomi had a rich relative called Boaz.

 2 The prophet Elijah once brought a dead person back to life, but the prophet Elisha did not.

 3 There were 13 tribes of Israel.

 4 When Miriam questioned Moses' leadership, she went blind.

 5 A woman called Rahab hid two Israelite spies on her roof in Jerusalem.

 6 After Adam and Eve had sinned, God sent angels to keep them out of the Garden of Eden.

 7 Esau sold his birthright to Jacob for a meal.

 8 The instrument David played for King Saul was a lyre.

 9 God sent the Israelites manna and sparrows to eat in the desert.

 10 The prophet Elisha once cured a Syrian army general of leprosy.

Initial Inquiry

QUESTION 5

For each question, the first letter
of the answer is given as a clue.

 1 Which 'J' was one of Joseph's brothers, who suggested selling him to slave traders?

 2 What 'L' were animals carved onto King Solomon's throne?

 3 Which 'M' was a desert tribe whose army turned on itself?

 4 Which 'J' was King Saul's son and David's best friend?

 5 Which 'H' appeared in the air at King Belshazzar's feast and wrote on a wall?

 6 Which 'D' was a king who had Bathsheba's husband killed so he could marry her?

 7 Which 'J' broke away from Israel and became a separate Jewish kingdom?

 8 Which 'E' means 'exit', and is the name of an Old Testament book?

9 What 'J' was the city in which King Solomon built many wonderful buildings?

QUESTION 10

 10 What 'V' is a place where grapes are grown, which Naboth owned, but King David wanted?

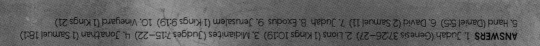

ANSWERS: 1. Judah (Genesis 37:26–27) **2.** Lions (1 Kings 10:19) **3.** Midianites (Judges 7:15–22) **4.** Jonathan (1 Samuel 18:1) **5.** Hand (Daniel 5:5) **6.** David (2 Samuel 11) **7.** Judah **8.** Exodus **9.** Jerusalem (1 Kings 9:19) **10.** Vineyard (1 Kings 21)

Anagram Antics

Read the clues and unscramble the
letters to work out the answers.

1. **cenad** — King David did this in celebration when the Ark of the Covenant came to Jerusalem.

2. **laab** — A false god worshipped by King Ahab, Queen Jezebel and their prophets.

3. **sebon** — Skeleton parts that the prophet Ezekiel once saw join together and come to life.

4. **squali** — Little birds that God sent to the Israelites to eat in the wilderness.

5. **sucer** — The opposite of 'bless', and the final word in the Old Testament.

6. **neevah** — The prophet Elijah travelled here in a chariot of fire.

7. **mafine** — Joseph predicted the crops would fail in Egypt, causing this.

8. **eseenz** — When the prophet Elisha brought a child back to life, the child did this seven times.

9. **eralsi** — This Jewish kingdom was conquered by the Assyrian empire.

10. **hudaj** — This Jewish kingdom was conquered by the Babylonian empire.

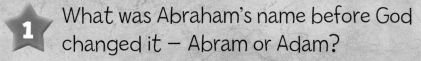

All About Abraham

Test how much you know about the father of God's people.

1 What was Abraham's name before God changed it — Abram or Adam?

2 What was Abraham's wife, Sarah, originally called — Naomi or Sarai?

3 What was Abraham's job — an animal farmer or a crop farmer?

4 What was the name of the nephew that Abraham adopted — Lot or Job?

Abraham

5 What was the name of Sarah's maid, with whom Abraham had a son — Hilda or Hagar?

6 What was this son's name — Ishmael or Ishtar?

7 Abraham also had a second son with his wife. What was this son's name — Isaiah or Isaac?

8 Who did God ask Abraham to sacrifice to him — his first or second son?

9 How long did it take Abraham to travel to the place of sacrifice — three weeks or three days?

10 How old was Abraham when he died — 75 or 175 years old?

ANSWERS 1. Abram (Genesis 12:1) 2. Sarai (Genesis 12:5) 3. An animal farmer (Genesis 13:2) 4. Lot (Genesis 12:5) 5. Hagar (Genesis 16:1) 6. Ishmael (Genesis 16:11) 7. Isaac (Genesis 21:4) 8. His second son, Isaac (Genesis 22) 9. Three days (Genesis 22:4) 10. 175 years old (Genesis 25:7)

38

Missing Words

Fill in the missing word in each of these quotations. The first letter is given for each.

1 "A land flowing with milk and h _ _ _ _ ."

2 "Go, lie down; and if he calls you, you shall say, 'Speak, Lord, for thy s _ _ _ _ _ _ hears.'"

3 "Your people shall be my people, and your G _ _ my G _ _ ."

4 "How are the mighty f _ _ _ _ _ in the midst of battle!"

5 "The Lord is my s _ _ _ _ _ _ _ , I shall not want."

6 "The price of w _ _ _ _ _ is above pearls."

7 "The Lord said to Cain, 'Where is Abel your brother?' He said, 'I do not know; am I my brother's k _ _ _ _ _ ?'"

8 "The fool says in his h _ _ _ _ , 'There is no God.'"

9 "For everything there is a season, and a time for every matter under H _ _ _ _ _ ."

10 "Then the Lord said to Moses, 'Go in to Pharaoh and say to him, "Thus says the Lord, 'Let my people g _ .'"

Heroes and Heroines

Test your knowledge of some of the Old Testament's most courageous men and women.

 1 Which Israelite was summoned by Deborah to lead an army against General Sisera — Barak or Balaam?

 2 For how many days did Esther fast before going to see the king — three or 13?

 3 Writing appeared at the feast of which king — Belshazzar or Nebuchadnezzar?

 4 How did Samson destroy the Philistines' temple — knocked it down or set fire to it?

 5 How did two midwives disobey the pharaoh — married Hebrew men or did not kill Hebrew baby boys?

 6 When Gideon spied on the Midianites, what did the thousands of warriors look like — ants or locusts?

 7 When General Sisera hid in a tent, which woman killed him — Jael or Jezebel?

 8 Which man was sent suffering by God but stayed faithful — Job or Jonah?

 9 What did the King of Persia reward Mordecai with — a palace or a parade?

 10 Who was Ruth's second husband — Mahlon or Boaz?

QUESTION 1

QUESTION 7

1 How many times did Samson lie to Delilah about the secret of his strength?

2 Which word can be used to describe Jonah, Elijah and Elisha?

3 Which tribe of Israel was King Saul from?

4 What is the word for an ancient type of paper used in the Old Testament?

5 Who became king of Israel after David?

6 What type of wood was King Solomon's Temple made from?

7 What is the name of the festival held to remember how Esther saved the Jews from destruction in Persia?

8 Where did God ask Jonah to go, to warn people to stop their wickedness?

9 How did Hannah ask God to send her a baby?

10 What tar-like material was smeared around the basket that baby Moses was left in, to make it watertight?

Place Puzzler

These questions are all about important places.

1 Which valley did Abraham's nephew Lot choose for farmland – the Jordan Valley or the Valley of Shechem?

2 Which cave did Abraham buy as a burial site – Adullam or Machpelah?

3 Which land in Egypt did Joseph give his family to live in – Gath or Goshen?

4 In which valley did Delilah live – the Valley of Sorek or the Valley of Salt?

5 Where did Cain go after he had killed Abel – the land of Nod or the land of Tob?

6 Where were the bodies of King Saul and his two sons found – Mount Gilboa or Mount Carmel?

7 Where was the Temple situated – the gardens of Babylon or Mount Zion?

8 Which was David's capital city before Jerusalem – Jericho or Hebron?

9 On which mountain did Moses receive the Ten Commandments – Sinai or Zion?

10 Which river did Jacob send his family across on the night he wrestled with God – Jabbok or Jordan?

Bible Baddies

Match these sinful people
with their nasty deeds.

1 Cain

A Disobeyed God

2 Korah

B Was an
   Israelite thief

3 Queen Jezebel

C Killed his brother,
   Abel

4 King Saul

D Captured and
   blinded Samson

5 Judah

E Ordered the Jews
   to be put to death

6 The Philistines

F Led a rebellion
   against Moses

7 Gehazi

G Was a champion of the
   Israelites' enemies

8 Achan

H Worshipped idols and
   practised witchcraft

9 Haman

I Sold his brother Joseph
   to passing traders

10 Goliath

J Was a dishonest servant
   to the prophet Elisha

Name Check

43

HARD

Answer each question using one of the names from the boxes below.

1. What did Gideon become known as after tearing down an altar of the false god Baal?
2. Whose name means 'he laughs'?
3. One pillar in the porch of Solomon's Temple was named Boaz – what was the other called?
4. What was the name of Moses' father-in-law?
5. The name of which of Jacob's sons means 'praise'?

Judah

Jerubbaal

Jethro

Isaac

Jakin

ANSWERS 1. Jerubbaal (Judges 6:25–32) 2. Isaac (Genesis 21:1–7) 3. Jakin (1 Kings 7:21) 4. Jethro (Exodus 3:1) 5. Judah (Genesis 29:35)

King or Prophet?

Read the clues to help you work out whether each of these men were kings or prophets.

1 **Amos** — Originally a sheep herder and sycamore fig farmer

2 **Habakkuk** — Openly questioned the wisdom of God

3 **Hezekiah** — A brave warrior who did not surrender to the Assyrians

4 **Jeremiah** — Tried to warn the people of Judah that they would be punished for worshipping false gods

5 **Joel** — Name means 'Jehovah is God'

6 **Rehoboam** — The son of King Solomon

7 **Nehemiah** — Tried to rebuild the walls of Jerusalem after it was conquered

8 **Omri** — Was once commander of the Israelite army

9 **Josiah** — Destroyed many altars to false gods

10 **Zachariah** — The son of King Jeroboam

Match these Biblical phrases with their modern interpretations.

1 "My cup runneth over" (Psalm 23:5)

2 "The writing on the wall" (Daniel 5)

3 "There's no peace for the wicked" (Isiah 57:21)

4 "To be one's brother's keeper" (Genesis 4:9)

5 "Holier than thou" (Isiah 65:5)

A Said when someone is under a lot of pressure

B Said to describe someone behaving in a superior way

C Said to describe a warning of coming failure

D Said when you accept responsibility for someone

E Said to express joy and good fortune

Multiple Choice

Select the correct answer from the three choices given.

 1 What was the name of Jacob's first wife?
a Lila **b** Leah **c** Lena

 2 Which of these objects were in Solomon's Temple?
a golden lampstands **b** silver basins **c** diamond cups

 3 Which of these was not a colour in Aaron's holy clothes?
a gold **b** purple **c** green

 4 Which king died by falling on his own sword?
a David **b** Saul **c** Solomon

 5 Which of these did the Queen of Sheba give Solomon?
a spices **b** silk **c** swords

 6 Which of these was the false god of the Philistines?
a Heber **b** Amos **c** Dagon

 7 Which of these was a friend of Job?
a Ahaziah **b** Bildad **c** Joash

 8 King Saul once tried to contact which dead prophet?
a Jonah **b** Elijah **c** Samuel

 9 What was the name of Jacob's daughter?
a Dinah **b** Delilah **c** Deborah

 10 Which of these was not an Israelite spy?
a Gaddiel **b** Gehazi **c** Geuel

Miracle Match-up

Match each person with the miracle that happened to them.

1 Joseph

2 Moses

3 Aaron

4 Balaam the soothsayer

5 Joshua

A God gave his donkey the power of speech

B God made the sun stand still, to help him win a battle

C Revealed the meaning of the pharaoh's dreams

D Had a staff which sprouted buds that blossomed into almonds

E Turned bitter water into sweet, drinkable water

QUESTION 4

HARD

48

Sum It Up

Use the references to look up the numbers and work out these maths problems.

1 Add together the length, width and height (in cubits) of the temple King Solomon built.

1 Kings 6:2

2 Subtract the number of days that God sent rain from the number of days that the flood waters lasted.

Genesis 7:12, Genesis 7:24

3 Add together the amount of prophets of the false god Baal and the false goddess Asherah.

1 Kings 18:19

4 Multiply the number of years by the number of months mentioned at the beginning of the Book of Ezekiel.

Ezekiel 1:1

5 Add together the total number of times that Joshua and the Israelites marched around Jericho.

Joshua 6:3-4

Expert Questions

See if you can answer these tricky
Old Testament questions.

1 People once tried to build the Tower of Gabble all the way up to Heaven — true or false?

2 Who built the golden calf for the Israelites to worship in the desert — Aaron or Miriam?

3 Which short Old Testament book is a collection of love poetry?

4 Which of Jacob's sons had a son called Muppim?
a Reuben **b** Joseph **c** Benjamin

5 Fill in the word missing from this quote: "You have been w _ _ _ _ _ _ in the balances and found wanting."

6 Select the correct spelling of this sinful city:
a Gormorah **b** Gomorrah **c** Gommora

7 What 'B' describes the appearance of the prophet Elisha?

8 **derbaoh** Unscramble the letters to find the only female Judge of Israel.

9 The kingdom of Judah broke away from the kingdom of Israel after the reign of which king — Solomon or David?

10 Which book of the Old Testament begins with 'O'?

50 Read and Remember

David and Goliath
(1 Samuel 17)

In Bethlehem, there lived an old man called Jesse who had eight sons. At the time, Saul was king of Israel, waging war against the fearsome Philistines who were constantly invading Israelite territory. Every Israelite man felt it was his duty to fight, and Jesse's three eldest sons had gone to join Saul's army. They had been away for several weeks and Jesse had heard nothing. One day, he packed some grain and bread for them, and ten cheeses as a gift for their commander. He gave these to his youngest son, David, to take to the battlefield. "Bring me word from your brothers," the old man urged.

Now David was just a young shepherd boy, but he rose early the next morning and set off alone to the frontline in the valley of Elah. He reached the army camp and his brothers just as the Israelites were marching onto the battlefield, preparing to fight the many rows of Philistines opposite them, yelling war cries. It was terrifying to see and hear. Suddenly, something even more frightening happened. The Philistine ranks parted and an enormous warrior came striding out from among them, taller than David had ever dreamed was possible! He wore huge, heavy armour and carried a massive bronze javelin and shield. "Why are you Israelites all lined up before me?" the giant bellowed. "I challenge you to send just one to fight me, Goliath of Gath, and if you win, we will all bow down before you!" He threw back his head and roared, and the Philistines smashed their spears against their shields in thunderous applause.

At that, the Israelite soldiers retreated. David was shocked. "Who is this man, that a whole army runs from him in fear?" Soldiers around him explained that this had been going on for several days. David was even more indignant. "He's putting us all to shame!" he exclaimed.

It didn't take long for news of the bold boy to reach King Saul. Saul wanted to see the little shepherd for himself and called David before him. To the king's great surprise, David volunteered to take up the giant's challenge and fight him!

"I've fought and killed bears and lions before, who have

attacked my sheep," countered David, "and I shall kill this Philistine just the same — God will protect me!"

Something about David's strength of faith convinced King Saul, and he agreed to let the shepherd boy try. He insisted on giving David his own armour to wear — but it was so big and bulky that David couldn't move in it, so had to take it off. King Saul and his army watched in amazement as David strode out to meet the giant warrior with just his staff, his slingshot and five smooth stones in his shepherd's pouch.

Goliath couldn't believe his eyes when he saw David marching towards him. He thought it must be a joke and roared with laughter.

"I come to you in the name of the Lord," David cried. "This day, he will deliver you into my hand, and all Philistines will tremble before him!"

Then the giant bellowed with fury and rushed towards David, preparing to deliver a death-blow with his javelin.

The shepherd boy stood firm. David reached into his pouch and took out a stone. He put it in his slingshot, whirled it around, and let it fly.

The stone hit the huge warrior in the middle of his

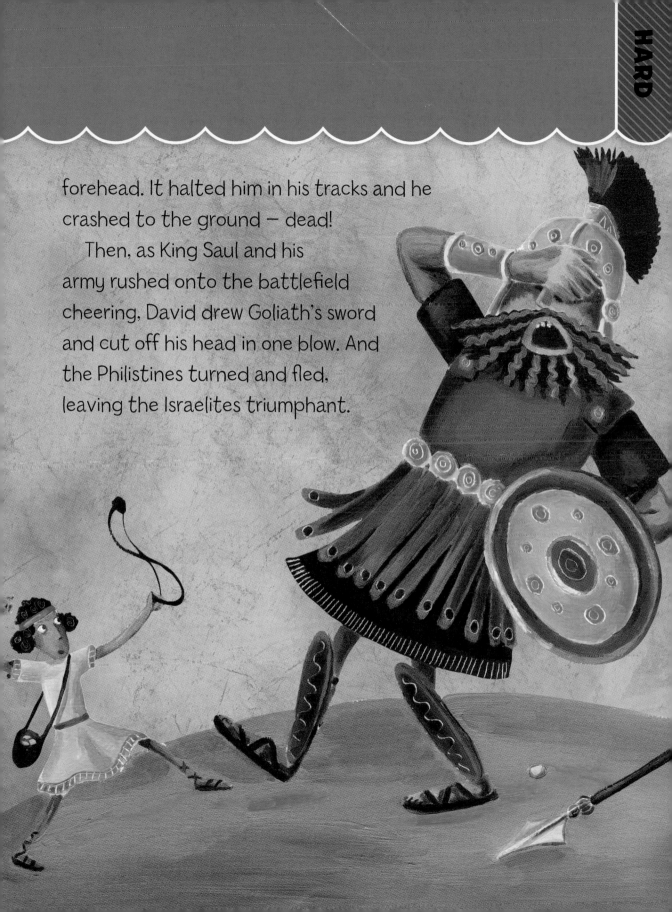

forehead. It halted him in his tracks and he crashed to the ground – dead!

Then, as King Saul and his army rushed onto the battlefield cheering, David drew Goliath's sword and cut off his head in one blow. And the Philistines turned and fled, leaving the Israelites triumphant.

Now, test your memory on what you have read by answering these questions.

 1 What was David's father's name?

 2 Where did he live?

 3 Where was the Israelite army camped?

 4 Where was Goliath from?

 5 What was Goliath carrying when he challenged the Israelites?

 6 What did the Israelites do when Goliath challenged them?

 7 Why didn't David wear King Saul's armour?

 8 Besides his slingshot and a pouch of stones, what did David carry when he went out to face Goliath?

 9 How many shots did David take to kill Goliath?

 10 What did the Philistines do when Goliath died?

New Testament

Get Going

Try these easy questions to get you started.

 1 Who was Jesus' father in Heaven?

 2 In which town was Jesus born?

 3 In which type of building was there no room for Mary and Joseph?

 4 How many men did Jesus choose to be his disciples?

 5 What was the job of several of Jesus' disciples?

 6 What is the word for the amazing feats that Jesus often performed?

 7 How many days passed before Jesus rose from the dead?

 8 Which of Jesus' disciples betrayed him?

 9 What food represented Jesus' body at the Last Supper?

 10 What are the first two words of the Lord's Prayer?

Who Am I?

Read the clues and look at the pictures for each person to work out who they are.

1 I was born in a stable. When I grew up, I taught people all about God. I died, but I came back to life.

2 I lived in Nazareth. I married a carpenter. I gave birth to a very special baby.

3 I was a carpenter. My wife had a baby who was the Son of God. An angel told me we were in danger, and that we should escape.

4 I was an important messenger sent from God. I appeared to a young woman. I told her that she would have a baby.

5 I preached about God. I prepared people for the coming of his son. I baptized many people in a river.

True or False?

Read these statements and decide whether they are true or false.

1. 'Hallowed be thy name' is a line from the Lord's Prayer.

2. Jesus brought dead people back to life.

3. Jesus once told a story about the perfect son.

4. The day before Jesus died, he had a last lunch with his disciples.

5. When Jesus was a boy, Mary and Joseph once lost him.

6. Jesus was put to death on a Saturday.

7. The holy seventh day of the week is known as the Sabbath.

8. Jesus once washed all the disciples' hands.

9. Jesus came back to life on the fifth day after he died.

10. Jesus was friendly to unpopular people, like tax collectors.

For each question, the first letter of the answer is given as a clue.

 1 What 'A' told shepherds about the birth of baby Jesus?

 2 What 'B' did Jesus bless and share at the Last Supper?

 3 What 'C' was Jesus made to wear on his head when he was put to death?

 4 What 'W' was often used by John the Baptist?

 5 What 'C' was Jesus put to death on?

6 What 'G' was the area where Jesus grew up?

 7 What 'K' was Herod, who wanted to kill baby Jesus?

 8 What 'C' is a huge group of people, such as often gathered around Jesus?

 9 What 'T' was the important building in Jerusalem where Jewish people prayed?

 10 What 'B' did Jesus sometimes cure?

QUESTION 2

QUESTION 7

Multiple Choice

Select the correct answer from
the three choices given.

1 Who did Jesus bring back from the dead?
a Lazarus **b** Peter **c** James

2 What did the wise men follow to find baby Jesus?
a an angel **b** a map **c** a star

3 Where did Jesus once calm a storm?
a the Red Sea **b** the river Nile **c** the Sea of Galilee

4 Who was Jesus baptized by?
a the angel Gabriel **b** Joseph **c** John the Baptist

5 Who tempted Jesus in the wilderness?
a John the Baptist **b** the devil **c** Moses

6 How did a tax collector manage to see Jesus in a crowd?
a stood on a donkey **b** climbed a tree **c** sat on a roof

7 Who is the 'Father' in the first line of the Lord's Prayer?
a your father **b** a priest **c** God

8 Who washed people's feet at the Last Supper?
a Judas **b** Jesus **c** John the Baptist

9 What did Jesus bless and share at the Last Supper?
a bread and wine **b** bread and water **c** bread and juice

10 Who was struck blind when he heard Jesus' voice?
a Peter **b** Stephen **c** Saul

ANSWERS: 1. a Lazarus (John 11:38–44) **2.** c A star (Matthew 2:2) **3.** c The Sea of Galilee (Luke 8:22–52) **4.** c John the Baptist (Matthew 3:13–14) **5.** b The devil (Matthew 4) **6.** b Climbed a tree (Luke 19:1–10) **7.** c God (Matthew 6:9) **8.** b Jesus (John 13:2–20) **9.** a Bread and wine (Mark 14:22–25) **10.** c Saul (Acts 9)

Read the clues and look at the picture hints to help you identify these animals.

1 I have four legs. Mary rode on me. I carried her to Bethlehem.

2 I have a snout. The prodigal son had a job looking after me. He was so hungry he almost ate my food!

3 I am a bird. One night, Peter denied knowing Jesus three times before I crowed at dawn. Peter then wept when he heard me.

4 I live in water. I was part of one of Jesus' miracles. He fed a crowd of five thousand with just two of me.

5 I am a wild animal. I was mentioned in the Sermon on the Mount. Jesus said false prophets are like me on the inside.

ANSWERS: 1. Donkey (Luke 15:15–17) 2. Pig (Luke 15:15–17) 3. Cock – cockerel/rooster (Matthew 26:34–35, 69–75) 4. Fish (Matthew 14:15–21) 5. Wolf (Matthew 7:15–16)

How Many?

All of these questions can be
answered with a number.

1 How many disciples did Jesus have?

2 How many days did Mary and Joseph search for Jesus
before finding him in the Temple in Jerusalem?

3 How many days and nights did Jesus spend fasting in
the wilderness?

4 How many bridesmaids were there in Jesus' parable
about bridesmaids who needed oil to light lamps?

5 How many loaves did Jesus once feed five thousand
people with?

6 How many times did the devil tempt Jesus in
the wilderness?

7 How many robbers were put to death alongside Jesus?

8 How many pieces of silver was Judas paid to
betray Jesus?

9 In the Good Samaritan story, how many people helped
the traveller who had been attacked?

10 How many gospels are there?

ANSWERS: 1. Twelve (Mark 3:13–19) **2.** Three (Luke 2:42) **3.** 40 (Matthew 4:2) **4.** Ten (Matthew 25:1–13) **5.** Five (Matthew 14:17) **6.** Three (Matthew 4) **7.** Two (Matthew 27:38) **8.** 30 (Matthew 26:15) **9.** One (Luke 10:25–37) **10.** Four

All About Mary

Test how much you know about the mother of Jesus.

1. Who told Mary she was going to have a baby — an angel or a doctor?

2. Who was Mary's husband — Joseph or Judas?

3. Who did Mary visit before her baby was born — her sister or her cousin?

4. What was the name of this relative — Eliza or Elizabeth?

Mary

5. What did an old man in the Temple tell Mary would one day pierce her soul — a sword or a spear?

6. During which Jewish festival did Mary and Joseph take the twelve-year-old Jesus to Jerusalem?

7. At what celebration did Mary ask Jesus to perform his first miracle — a birthday party or a wedding?

8. What did Mary watch Jesus do as his first miracle — change stones into bread or change water into wine?

9. When Jesus was dying on the cross, where was Mary — at home or standing nearby?

10. When Jesus was dying, whom did he ask to look after Mary — Peter or John?

ANSWERS: 1. An angel (Luke 1:26) 2. Joseph (Luke 1:27) 3. Her cousin (Luke 1:36–41) 4. Elizabeth (Luke 1:36) 5. A sword (Luke 2:35) 6. Passover (Luke 2:41) 7. A wedding (John 2:1–11) 8. Change water into wine (John 2:1–11) 9. Standing nearby (John 19:25) 10. John – the disciple whom he loved (John 19:26–27)

59

Anagram Antics

Read the clues and unscramble the letters to work out the answers.

 1 yarm   Jesus' mother.

 2 dogl   One of the gifts the wise men brought for baby Jesus.

 3 oved   The Spirit of God appeared when Jesus was baptized, in the form of this bird.

 4 isns   Jesus said he had the power to forgive these.

 5 nsorht   The crown Jesus was made to wear when he was put to death was made of these.

 6 tabo   The disciples were in this when Jesus came walking to them on the surface of the water.

 7 karm   One of the gospel writers.

 8 pyra   What Jesus went to a garden to do, the night before he died.

 9 ocni   Jesus told a story about a widow who lost one of these, but swept the house until she found it.

 10 honj   Jesus' cousin.

ANSWERS: 1. Mary (Luke 1:30–31) **2.** Gold (Matthew 2:11) **3.** Dove (Matthew 3:16) **4.** Sins (Matthew 2:10) **5.** Thorns (Mark 15:17) **6.** Boat (Mark 6:47–48) **7.** Mark **8.** Pray (Matthew 26:36–40) **9.** Coin (Luke 15:8–10) **10.** John (Luke 1, 2)

Place Puzzler

These questions are all about important places.

 1 Where was Joseph born — Bethany or Bethlehem?

 2 Where did Jesus grow up — Nazareth or Jerusalem?

 3 Where did John the Baptist preach — in the desert or in a city?

 4 Where was Jesus baptized — in a river or in the sea?

QUESTION 4

5 When King Herod wanted to kill Jesus, which country did Joseph take Mary and Jesus to — Lebanon or Egypt?

 6 Which direction did the wise men who visited Jesus come from — the east or the west?

 7 Which city did Jesus enter on a donkey — Jerusalem or Jericho?

QUESTION 10

8 Where did the Last Supper take place — in a house or in a garden?

 9 Where was Jesus' body laid to rest — in a grave or in a tomb?

 10 Where was Saul travelling to when he was struck blind by Jesus' voice — Emmaus or Damascus?

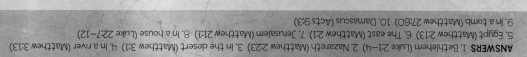

ANSWERS 1. Bethlehem (Luke 2:1–4) 2. Nazareth (Matthew 2:23) 3. In the desert (Matthew 3:1) 4. In a river (Matthew 3:13) 5. Egypt (Matthew 2:13) 6. The east (Matthew 2:1) 7. Jerusalem (Matthew 21:1) 8. In a house (Luke 22:7–12) 9. In a tomb (Matthew 27:60) 10. Damascus (Acts 9:3)

Testing Trivia

Test your general New Testament knowledge.

EASY

61

1 What did Mary place Jesus in when he was born?

2 In which city was Jesus put to death?

3 Who did Jesus cure first at Capernaum?

4 What was the name of the man whose daughter Jesus brought back to life?

5 Who ordered John the Baptist to be put in prison?

6 In the Good Samaritan story, who was the first person to pass by the traveller who had been attacked?

7 Which disciple was the brother of James?

8 In which river was Jesus baptized?

9 How many of Jesus' disciples were originally named Simon?

10 What is the name of the religion that Jesus followed?

Test how much you know about the time
when Jesus died and came back to life.

1 What colour was the robe that the Roman soldiers dressed Jesus in — purple or white?

2 When Jesus was praying in the garden, what did his friends do — talk or sleep?

QUESTION 2

3 What was the name of the garden — Gethsemane or Galilee?

4 What did the Roman soldiers cast lots for — Jesus' clothes or his donkey?

5 How many hours of darkness were there while Jesus hung on the cross — three or four?

6 Who requested the tomb to be sealed — Jesus' friends or the chief priests and Pharisees?

7 After Jesus' crucifixion, who asked for his body — Joseph of Arimathea or Peter?

QUESTION 10

8 Which gospel mentions that Jesus' tomb was sealed — Matthew or John?

9 On Easter Sunday morning, who rolled the stone away — Mary or an angel?

10 To whom did Jesus first appear after he rose from the dead — Peter or Mary Magdalene?

ANSWERS 1. Purple (Mark 15:17) **2.** Sleep (Mark 14:37–41) **3.** Gethsemane (Mark 14:32) **4.** Jesus' clothes (John 19:23–24) **5.** Three (Luke 23:44) **6.** The chief priests and Pharisees (Matthew 27:62–66) **7.** Joseph of Arimathea (Mark 15:42–43) **8.** Matthew (Matthew 27:62–66) **9.** An angel (Matthew 28:2) **10.** Mary Magdalene (Mark 16:9)

Missing Link

Complete each statement using one
of the words from the boxes below.

1 The gospel writers were Matthew, Mark, Luke
and _ _ _ _ .

2 Jesus cured people who were lepers, blind
and _ _ _ _ _ _ _ _ _ .

3 Three of Jesus' parables were the good Samaritan, the
prodigal son and the lost _ _ _ _ .

4 People whom Jesus said were blessed included the meek,
the merciful, and the pure in _ _ _ _ _ .

5 Followers of Jesus who spread the word of God after his
death included Peter, Stephen and _ _ _ _ .

coin

paralyzed

heart

Paul

John

Family Connections

Match these family members with
their relationship to each other.

 1 Mary and Jesus

 2 Zechariah and Elizabeth

 3 Jesus and John the Baptist

 4 Mary, Martha and Lazarus

 5 King Herod and Salome

QUESTION 1

 A Cousins

 B Siblings

 C Husband and wife

 D Step-father and step-daughter

 E Mother and son

QUESTION 5

EASY

65

Read and Remember

Read this short story and try to
remember as much as you can.

The Birth of Jesus
(Matthew 1:18–25, Luke 2:1–24)

In the town of Nazareth, a young woman called Mary was engaged to a carpenter, Joseph. One day, the angel Gabriel appeared to Mary. "Do not be afraid," he said. "You are going to have a baby who will be the Son of God. He is to be called Jesus." An angel also appeared to Joseph, and told him that he should not be afraid to take Mary as his wife. They were soon married.

However, as the time drew near when the baby was to be born, the Roman emperor Augustus Caesar decided there should be a survey of all the people in his lands. He sent out an order saying that every man had to travel to the place where he was born. Joseph had been born in the city of Bethlehem in Judea, so that was where he and Mary had to go. It was a long, tiring journey — especially for Mary, who was heavily pregnant.

When the couple finally reached Bethlehem,

the city was so full of travellers who, like them, had arrived to be registered that they could find nowhere to stay. Fortunately, a kindly innkeeper allowed them to shelter in his stable. That was where baby Jesus was born, that night, among the animals. Mary wrapped him in cloth and laid him in a manger full of straw.

In the fields outside the city, shepherds were watching over their flocks. Suddenly, the night sky blazed with light and an angel appeared. The shepherds were terrified! But the angel spoke gently, saying, "Do not be afraid, for I bring wonderful news. This very night a child has been born who will be the saviour of all people. You can find him in a stable in Bethlehem, lying in a manger." Then all at once the heavens were filled with thousands of angels. "Glory to God – and peace to all people!" they sang. The shepherds were amazed, and hurried straight to Bethlehem.

The shepherds soon found the stable, and the manger, and the baby who was to be the saviour of the world, just as the angels had said. They praised God and gave thanks for the wonderful things that had happened.

Now, test your memory on what you have read by answering these questions.

 1 Where did Joseph and Mary live?

 2 Who told Mary that she would have a baby?

 3 Which emperor ordered a survey of all the people in his lands?

 4 Where had Joseph been born?

 5 Who offered Mary and Joseph shelter?

 6 What type of building was Jesus born in?

 7 What time of day was Jesus born?

 8 What did Mary use as a bed for baby Jesus?

 9 Who were the first people to be told that the saviour had been born?

 10 What did the angels sing?

66

True or False?

Read these statements and decide
whether they are true or false.

1 Jesus often taught people about God through songs.

2 The wise men who visited baby Jesus were warned in a dream not to return to King Herod.

3 The Jewish tribe that Jesus was descended from was called Judah.

4 John the Baptist's clothes were made of camel hair.

5 Jesus was walking by the Sea of Galilee when he called his first disciples.

6 Peter was from a city called Bethsaida.

7 Jesus once fed 5000 people with five fish and two loaves of bread.

8 While Jesus was alive, he appeared to Peter, James and John, talking to Moses and Elijah.

9 When Jesus entered Jerusalem on the week of his death, he rode a camel.

10 One of the gospels was written by Jesus.

Read the clues and look at the pictures for
each person to work out who they are.

1 I was originally called Saul. While travelling along a road, God spoke to me, and I became a Christian. I was once shipwrecked.

2 I committed sins. I was Jesus' close friend. I was the first person to see him after he rose from the dead.

3 I was one of Jesus' disciples. My name was originally Simon. I was put in prison for being a Christian.

4 I had a sister called Mary. Jesus visited our house. I worried about all the work I had to do, while Mary listened to Jesus.

5 I was a tax collector. I lived in Jericho. I was short and so I had to climb a tree to see Jesus amongst a crowd.

68

How Many?

All of these questions can be answered with a number.

1 How many days was Lazarus in his tomb before being brought back to life by Jesus?

2 Jesus sent his disciples out to preach in groups of how many?

3 Jesus once praised a poor widow for giving all her money to the Temple. How many coins did she give?

4 How many days was Saul blind for after he heard Jesus' voice while on the road to Damascus?

5 How many baskets of leftover food were there when Jesus fed the 5000?

6 How many legions of angels did Jesus say God would send him if he asked?

7 How many times did Peter deny that he knew Jesus before the cock crowed?

8 In the parable of the lost sheep, how many sheep did the shepherd count safely into the fold?

9 How many of his disciples did Jesus ask to watch over him while he prayed in the Garden of Gethsemane?

10 For how many days was Jesus seen by the disciples before ascending to Heaven?

Initial Inquiry

69

MEDIUM

For each question, the first letter
of the answer is given as a clue.

1 Which 'A' is a book in the
New Testament?

2 What 'H' is a word used to welcome
Jesus as he entered Jerusalem?

3 What 'P' were the kind of branches
that the crowd welcomed Jesus with?

QUESTION 3

4 What 'S' was the kind of tree that
Zacchaeus climbed in order to see Jesus?

5 What 'W' was the colour that Jesus' clothes became
when he appeared, speaking to Moses and Elijah?

6 What 'A' was the name of a prophetess who was in the
Temple when Mary and Joseph presented baby Jesus?

7 What 'C' were people whom Jesus
welcomed to him?

QUESTION 7

8 What 'F' was a tree that Jesus cursed
when it had no fruit on it?

9 Which 'B' was the name of one of Jesus'
twelve disciples?

10 What 'S' was a man to whom God promised
that before he died he would see Christ?

ANSWERS: 1. Acts **2.** Hosanna (John 12:13) **3.** Palm (John 12:13) **4.** Sycamore (Luke 19:1–10) **5.** White (Mark 9:3) **6.** Anna (Luke 2:36–38) **7.** Children (Matthew 19:14) **8.** Fig (Matthew 21:19) **9.** Bartholomew (Matthew 10:3) **10.** Simeon (Luke 2:25–35)

Anagram Antics

Read the clues and unscramble the
letters to work out the answers.

1 nestos — The devil tempted Jesus to turn these into loaves of bread.

2 nglesa — These appeared to shepherds on the night that Jesus was born.

3 axste — Matthew was a collector of these before he became a disciple.

4 velois — The name of the mountain where the Garden of Gethsemane was situated.

5 verpi — Jesus said that the Pharisees were like a brood of this type of snake.

6 odtcor — This was believed to be the profession of the gospel writer Luke.

7 dmub — Unable to speak — like Zechariah, when he did not believe an angel.

8 almta — A ship that Paul was travelling on was wrecked off the coast of this island.

9 strich — A name for Jesus, used to show that he was God's chosen one.

10 name — The final word in the New Testament.

Answer these questions about significant signs and symbols.

1 At Pentecost, what sign of the Holy Spirit hovered over the disciples – a dove or a tongue of fire?

2 What did Jesus say he was – the light of the world or the light of Heaven?

3 How did Judas tell the guards who Jesus was – kissed him or tapped him?

QUESTION 4

4 At the Last Supper, what symbolized Jesus' blood – water or wine?

5 What did the sign on Jesus' cross refer to him as – 'the King of the Jews' or 'the Son of God'?

6 As a sign that the disciples should always care for others, what did Jesus wash – their hands or their feet?

7 What plant did Jesus use as a symbol for himself – a vine or a fig tree?

QUESTION 10

8 What did Paul describe the Church as – Christ's house or Christ's body?

9 What convinced Thomas that Jesus had risen – Jesus' tomb or his wounds?

10 God sent Peter a vision of creatures on a sheet as a sign to baptize who – animals or non-Jews?

ANSWERS 1. A tongue of fire (Acts 2:3) **2.** The light of the world (John 8:12) **3.** Judas kissed Jesus (Mark 14:43–52) **4.** Wine (Matthew 26:27–29) **5.** The King of the Jews (John 19:20) **6.** Jesus washed their feet (John 13:1–17) **7.** A vine (John 15) **8.** Christ's body (1 Corinthians 12:12) **9.** The wounds in Jesus' hands, feet and side (John 20:25) **10.** Non-Jews – Gentiles (Acts 10)

Testing Trivia

Test your general New Testament knowledge.

1 What are the names of the four gospels?

2 What did the disciples become known as after Jesus' death?

3 What is the name often used for the story of the first Christmas — Jesus' birth?

4 When Jesus threw people out of the Temple in Jerusalem, what did he say it had been turned into?

5 What name is the disciple Bartholomew called in John's gospel?

6 Which of the disciples swam to reach Jesus when he appeared to them after the resurrection?

7 When Jesus compared himself to a good shepherd, what did he say he would do for his sheep?

8 Who did Jesus say that you should love as you love yourself?

9 At Pentecost in Jerusalem there were Jews from every what?

10 In the Lord's Prayer, which word follows 'Hallowed be thy ...'?

What Am I?

Read the clues and look at the picture
hints to help you identify these animals.

73

MEDIUM

1 I am a plant-eating insect. John the
Baptist ate me in the desert. I am also
in a prophecy in the book of Revelation.

2 I am a small bird. Jesus said God does
not forget me. He said his disciples were
more important than many of me.

3 I am a huge animal. Jesus reminded people that
Jonah was trapped inside me for three days.
He compared this to his resurrection.

4 I have a sting. I am mentioned after the
Lord's prayer. Jesus said that a father
would not give me as a gift to his child.

5 I breathe fire. I am mentioned in the last
book of the New Testament, Revelation.
I represent the devil.

Multiple Choice

Select the correct answer from
the three choices given.

1 Who was the father of James and John?
a Zebedee **b** Zechariah **c** Zacchaeus

2 What type of illness did Peter's mother-in-law have?
a leprosy **b** a fever **c** toothache

3 What does 'Golgotha', where Jesus was crucified, mean?
a place of death **b** place of the skull **c** gathering place

4 What was Judas' surname?
a Iscariot **b** Levi **c** Cornelius

5 Which of these is not something Jesus cured?
a bleeding **b** a withered hand **c** stuttering

6 Who looked after the twelve disciples' money?
a Peter **b** Judas **c** Jesus

7 How many demons were cast out of Mary Magdalene?
a five **b** six **c** seven

8 Who was Jesus taken to after his arrest?
a the high priest **b** the Roman governor **c** the king

9 After Jesus died, who was first to perform a miracle?
a Peter **b** John **c** Paul

10 What did Pontius Pilate wash in front of everyone?
a his robe **b** his face **c** his hands

Test how much you know
about the Son of God.

1 At what age did Jesus begin teaching about God – 20 or 30?

2 What did Jesus do for 40 days in the wilderness – fast or preach?

3 What were Jesus' last words on the cross – 'It is done' or 'It is finished'?

4 Where was Jesus presented after he was born – the stable or the Temple?

5 Matthew's gospel calls Jesus 'Emmanuel'. Does this mean 'God is with us' or 'This man does well'?

6 When Mary and Joseph found Jesus in the Temple, who was he talking to – disciples or teachers?

7 On which day of the week did Jesus enter Jerusalem before his death – Sunday or Tuesday?

8 Who did Jesus throw out of the Temple in Jerusalem – Pharisees and Sadducees or moneylenders and traders?

9 When Jesus calmed the storm, what was this a sign of – his power over nature or his power over demons?

10 How did Jesus go up to Heaven – was he swept away by a whirlwind or did he disappear into the clouds?

Jesus

ANSWERS 1. 30 (Luke 3:23) 2. Fast (Matthew 4:1–2) 3. 'It is finished' (John 19:30) 4. The Temple (Luke 2:27) 5. 'God is with us' (Matthew 1:23–24) 6. Teachers (Luke 2:45–47) 7. Sunday (Mark 11:1–11) 8. Moneylenders and traders (Matthew 21:12) 9. His power over nature (Matthew 8:23–27) 10. He disappeared into the clouds (Acts 1:9)

1 Jesus' followers:
a disciples **b** discipels **c** disiples

2 The garden in which Jesus prayed before he died:
a Gethsemene **b** Gethsemane **c** Gethsemany

3 People who became some of the first Christians:
a Phillipians **b** Philipians **c** Philippians

4 A fishing village on the shore of the Sea of Galilee:
a Capernaum **b** Capernum **c** Capernam

5 A Jewish place of worship:
a sinagogue **b** synagogue **c** synnagogue

6 A group of Jews who were rich and held important jobs:
a Saduccees **b** Sadduccees **c** Sadducees

7 The way in which Jesus was put to death on the cross:
a crucifiction **b** crucificion **c** crucifixion

8 The name for Jesus' followers after his death:
a appostle **b** apostle **c** apostel

9 A city where people became some of the first Christians:
a Thessalonia **b** Thesalonia **c** Thesalonnia

10 A Hebrew word that means 'God's chosen one':
a Massiah **b** Messiah **c** Mesiah

Risen!

Test how much you know about the days after Jesus rose from the dead.

77

MEDIUM

1. Two disciples spoke with Jesus without realizing, on a road to where — Damascus or Emmaus?

2. How many days after his death did Jesus ascend into Heaven — 14 or 40?

QUESTION 1

3. Who watched Jesus ascend, along with the disciples — soldiers or angels?

4. How many days after Jesus' death did Pentecost take place — 30 or 50?

5. Who did Jesus say would remind the disciples of his teachings — his mother, Mary, or the Holy Ghost?

6. To prove to the disciples that he wasn't a ghost, what did Jesus eat — bread or fish?

7. From where did Jesus ascend — the Mount of Olives or Mount Sinai?

QUESTION 7

8. To whom did Jesus say 'feed my sheep' — Peter or Paul?

9. At Pentecost, what filled the disciples' room — a rushing wind or a fiery heat?

10. The Holy Spirit made the disciples expert at what — telling stories or speaking different languages?

Timeline Teaser

Test yourself on the order of
New Testament events.

1 Who was born first – John the Baptist or Jesus?

2 Which happened first – the shepherds' visit to baby Jesus, or the presentation of Jesus in the Temple?

3 Which happened first – Jesus' baptism or his temptation in the wilderness?

4 Which did Jesus do first – turn water into wine, or calm a storm?

5 Which happened first – Jesus foretelling his own death to the disciples or the death of John the Baptist?

6 Which did Jesus do first – ride a donkey into Jerusalem, or give the Sermon on the Mount?

7 Which did Jesus do first – pray in the Garden of Gethsemane or hold the Last Supper?

8 Which happened first – Peter's denial of Jesus or Judas' betrayal of Jesus?

9 Which happened first – Peter's imprisonment or Jesus' ascension into Heaven?

10 Which happened first – the death of Stephen or Saul's vision on the road to Damascus?

Find the missing name in these
well-known pairs.

1 Elizabeth and _ _ _ _ _ _ _ _ _

2 Peter and _ _ _ _ _ _

QUESTION 2

3 James and _ _ _ _

4 Martha and _ _ _ _

5 Aquila and _ _ _ _ _ _ _ _ _

QUESTION 7

6 Anna and _ _ _ _ _ _

7 Mary and _ _ _ _ _ _

8 Paul and _ _ _ _ _

9 Ananias and _ _ _ _ _ _ _ _

10 Cornelius and _ _ _ _ _

ANSWERS 1. Zechariah 2. Andrew 3. John 4. Mary 5. Priscilla 6. Simeon 7. Joseph 8. Silas 9. Sapphira 10. Peter

MEDIUM

80

Books Bamboozler

Decide whether each of these statements about the books of the New Testament is true or false.

1 There are 27 books in the New Testament.

2 The shortest book in the New Testament is the Second Letter of John.

3 The Book of Revelation tells the story of the birth of Jesus.

4 Acts is about Jesus' miracles.

5 Paul wrote at least 13 books of the New Testament.

6 Lamentations is a New Testament book.

7 Acts is believed to have been written by Luke.

8 There is a New Testament book called Judas.

9 The Beatitudes (Jesus' pronouncements about people who are blessed) are found in the Gospel of Matthew.

10 There are 21 New Testament books that are letters (epistles).

Read and Remember

Read this short story and try to
remember as much as you can.

81

MEDIUM

Jesus Walks on Water
(Matthew 14:22–33, Mark 6:45–52, John 6:5–21)

It was the end of a long day for Jesus and his disciples at the shore of the Sea of Galilee. An enormous crowd of thousands of people had gathered there, and so Jesus had talked to them all day, performing miracles too. Everyone was reluctant to leave. Jesus turned to his weary disciples.

"It's going to take me a little while to convince everyone to leave," Jesus explained to them, as night began to draw in. "Take the boat and go ahead without me. I'll see all the people off and then I want to go up to the mountainside for a while and spend some time praying on my own. I'll meet you later."

The disciples must have wondered how Jesus was going to catch them up, but they did as they were told. They clambered aboard a little fishing boat and cast off towards the far shore, for Capernaum, where they were going to stay that night.

As the men sailed away, Jesus turned back to the crowds and told them it was time to go home too.

Then he went a little way up a hillside. He stayed for quite a while, deep in thought, talking to God.

By the time the disciples had reached the middle of the lake, they were in deep trouble. A sudden storm had picked up and strong winds were battering the boat. Hours passed and the night grew darker, the wind grew wilder and the waves grew higher. Several of the disciples were experienced sailors, but they couldn't stop the boat from being buffeted off course. The disciples were very frightened.

As they sat huddled in the boat, desperately waiting for the light of dawn, they spotted a white glow in the darkness. It came nearer and grew bigger, until it looked like a man walking on the water. "A ghost!" they cried, even more terrified than before.

Then a voice reached them across the water. "Take heart – it's me, Jesus. Don't be afraid!"

The disciples looked at each other in astonishment.

Peter bravely called out, "If it's really you, Lord, tell me to come to you."

"Come," said the figure, holding out his hand.

The other disciples held their breath as Peter

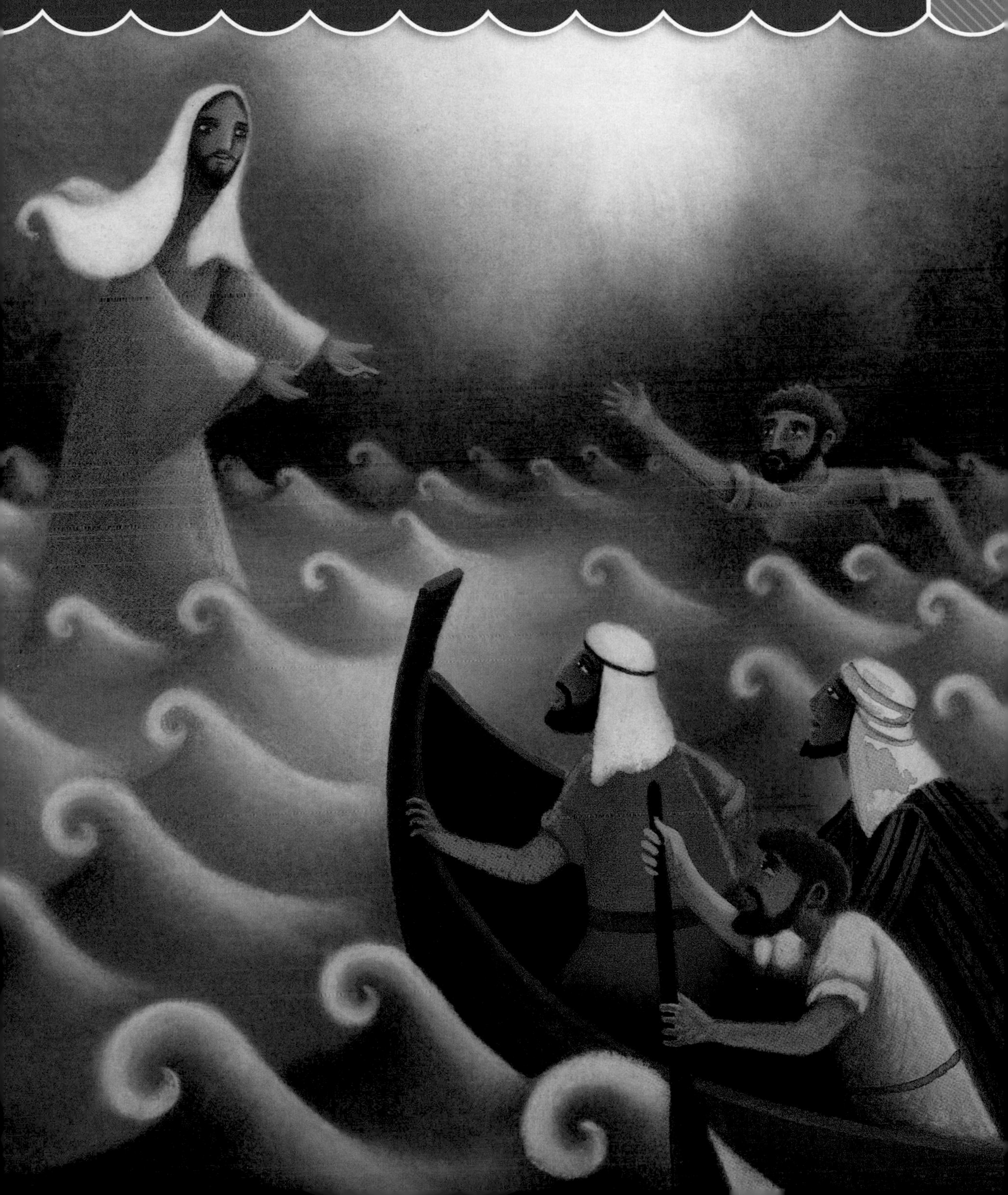

stood up in the rocking boat and stepped out.

They could hardly believe their eyes as they watched Peter walk across the waves, closer and closer to Jesus. He kept his eyes fixed on Jesus all the time, but just as he had nearly reached him, he dared to look down. The moment he saw the churning depths beneath his feet, his belief faltered, his courage deserted him and he plunged down into the foam.

"Help me, Jesus!" Peter screamed in panic. Immediately, Jesus grabbed him and hauled him back up. "Why did you suddenly have doubt?" he scolded gently, helping Peter back to the boat.

As soon as Jesus had rejoined the disciples, the wind ceased and the waves died down.

The disciples were amazed. "Truly, you are the Son of God," they gasped in wonder.

Now, test your memory on what you have read by answering these questions.

1 Where were Jesus and the disciples?

2 What did Jesus want to do, after all the people had gone?

3 What type of boat did the disciples get into?

4 Where were Jesus and the disciples going to stay that night?

5 What caused the boat to go off course?

6 What did the disciples see in the darkness?

7 What did they think at first was coming towards them on the waves?

8 Why did Peter suddenly fall into the sea?

9 What happened as soon as Jesus reached the boat with Peter?

10 After witnessing these extraordinary events, what did the disciples decide about Jesus?

ANSWERS 1. At the shore of the Sea of Galilee **2.** Go up a mountainside and pray **3.** A little fishing boat **4.** Capernaum **5.** A storm **6.** A white glow **7.** A ghost **8.** He looked down and his belief faltered **9.** The storm died down **10.** That he truly was the Son of God

82 Famous Firsts

Answer these questions about firsts in the New Testament.

1 What is the first book of the New Testament?

2 According to John's gospel, where did Jesus perform his first miracle — Cana or Capernaum?

3 Who was the first Christian martyr (a person who is killed because of their beliefs) — Saul or Stephen?

4 Nine sentences in the Sermon on the Mount had which first two words — 'Blessed are' or 'Praise be'?

5 What did Jesus first say to the disciples after his resurrection — 'Do not be afraid' or 'Peace be with you'?

6 Who was the first Gentile (non-Jew) to be baptized as a follower of Jesus — Pontius Pilate or Cornelius?

7 What are the first words of John's Gospel — 'In the beginning was God' or 'In the beginning was the Word'?

8 Where did Mary Magdalene go on the first day of the week after Jesus' death — to his tomb or the Temple?

9 What did Jesus say we should 'seek first' — God's kingdom and his righteousness or our daily bread?

10 In which book are these the first words: 'In the first book, O Theophilus...' — Acts or Revelation?

Who Am I?

Read the clues and look at the pictures for each person to work out who they are.

 1 I was a priest. An angel told me I would have a son. I did not believe it so the angel struck me dumb.

 **2** I lived in Jericho. I was a blind beggar. I had faith in Jesus, and he restored my sight.

 3 I was a Roman Centurion (commander) in Caesaria. I was committed to worshipping God. Peter baptized me.

 **4** I was one of Jesus' disciples. I was doubtful that Jesus had risen from the dead. When I saw his wounds, I believed.

 5 I was a Roman governor. The Jewish elders demanded that I sentence Jesus to death. I did not want to be responsible for it.

84 True or False?

Read these statements and decide whether they are true or false.

1 The prophetess Anna was 94 years old when she saw baby Jesus in the Temple.

2 On his missionary journeys, Paul hoped to visit Spain.

3 Jesus appeared on a mountain speaking with Moses and Abraham.

4 Lazarus, Mary and Martha lived at Bethany.

5 Matthew worked for the Romans before he became a disciple.

6 Three soldiers crucified Jesus.

7 When the Prodigal Son returned, his father gave him a golden chain.

8 In Lystra, Paul and Barnabas were worshipped as gods after Paul healed a man who could not walk.

9 When Jesus was in the house of Simon the Leper, a woman anointed him with a special perfume called nard.

10 Jesus once told a parable about five bridesmaids.

ANSWERS: 1. False – she was 84 (Luke 2:37) **2.** True (Romans 15:24) **3.** False – it was Moses and Elijah (Matthew 17:3) **4.** True (John 11) **5.** True (Matthew 9:9) **6.** False – it was four (John 19:23) **7.** False – his father gave him a ring (Luke 15:22) **8.** True (Acts 14:8–12) **9.** True (Mark 14:3) **10.** False – it was ten bridesmaids (Matthew 25:1–13)

Initial Inquiry

For each question, the first letter
of the answer is given as a clue.

1 Which 'E' was a natural disaster which helped to release Paul and Silas from prison?

2 What 'B' was the prisoner the people wanted released instead of Jesus?

3 Which 'J' was a man whose daughter Jesus brought back to life?

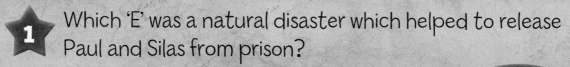

4 What 'H' did Mary use to wipe Jesus' feet after anointing them with perfume?

5 Which 'S' was the day on which Jesus healed a man's withered hand and so angered the Jewish elders?

6 What 'B' was the meal that the risen Jesus cooked for Peter and other disciples at the Sea of Tiberias?

7 What 'L' was the name of a dealer in purple cloth at Philippi?

QUESTION 7

8 Which 'M' mistook the risen Jesus for a gardener?

9 What 'P' ran into the sea and drowned when Jesus cast demons into them?

10 What 'C' was the chief priest on whose orders Jesus was arrested?

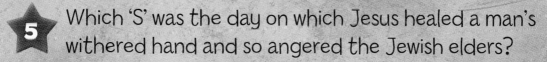

ANSWERS 1. Earthquake (Acts 16:26) 2. Barabbas (Matthew 27:15–26) 3. Jairus (Mark 5:35–43) 4. Hair (John 12:3) 5. Sabbath (Mark 3:1–6) 6. Breakfast (John 21:15) 7. Lydia (Acts 16:14) 8. Mary Magdalene (John 20:15) 9. Pigs (Matthew 8:28–34) 10. Caiaphas (Matthew 26:57)

HARD

86

Anagram Antics

Read the clues and unscramble the letters to work out the answers.

1 astlspoe — The name by which the twelve disciples became known after Jesus' death.

2 ynagsogue — A Jewish place of worship.

3 hilpip — One of Jesus' disciples.

4 ritanuc — In the Temple, this piece of material was torn in two when Jesus died.

5 dustram — Jesus said if you have faith as small as this seed, you could move a mountain.

6 mabsphley — The charge on which the Jewish court sentenced Jesus to death.

7 sadrenks — This covered the land for three hours while Jesus was dying on the cross.

8 teepsontc — The Jewish festival during which the Holy Spirit visited the disciples.

9 staan — A name used in the New Testament for the devil.

10 amdsausc — The city that Saul was on his way to when he heard Jesus' voice.

ANSWERS: 1. Apostles (Acts 1:1–12) 2. Synagogue (Luke 4:14–21) 3. Philip (Mark 3:18) 4. Curtain (Mark 15:38) 5. Mustard (Matthew 17:20) 6. Blasphemy (John 19:7) 7. Darkness (Luke 23:44–45) 8. Pentecost (Acts 2:1–4) 9. Satan (Matthew 4:10) 10. Damascus (Acts 9:1–9)

All About Peter

Test how much you know about this 'fisher of men'.

Peter

1 Jesus said Peter was the rock on which he would build his what — house or church?

2 Which weapon did Peter use to defend Jesus — a sword or a spear?

3 Who was Peter's brother — Andrew or John?

4 Who did Peter bring back from the dead — Tabitha or Lydia?

5 What injury did Peter do to a servant of the high priest — broke his arm or cut off his ear?

6 What did Peter at first refuse to let Jesus do at the Last Supper — lay the table or wash Peter's feet?

7 How many times did Peter deny knowing Jesus after his arrest?

8 When Peter was fishing, and he saw the risen Jesus on the shore, how did he reach him — rowing or swimming?

9 When Peter was imprisoned in Jerusalem by King Herod, who helped him escape — an angel or a Roman guard?

10 When asked by Jesus who people thought he was, what did Peter say — 'You are the Christ' or 'You are truth'?

Missing Words

Fill in the missing word in each of these quotations. The first letter is given for each.

1 "Henceforth all generations will call me b _ _ _ _ _ _ _ ; for he who is mighty has done great things for me."

2 "This is my beloved S _ _ , with whom I am well pleased."

3 "He who is coming after me is mightier than I, whose s _ _ _ _ _ _ _ I am not worthy to carry."

4 "If any man would come after me, let him deny himself and take up his c _ _ _ _ and follow me."

5 "Truly, I say to you, today you will be with me in P _ _ _ _ _ _ _ _ ."

6 "Enter by the narrow g _ _ _ , for the g _ _ _ is wide and the way is easy that leads to destruction."

7 "I see men; but they look like t _ _ _ _ _ , walking."

8 "For by one S _ _ _ _ _ _ we were all baptized into one body — Jews or Greeks, slaves or free."

9 "Blessed are those who mourn, for they shall be c _ _ _ _ _ _ _ _ _ ."

10 "My God, my God, why hast thou f _ _ _ _ _ _ _ _ me?"

Heroes and Heroines

Test your knowledge of some of the New Testament's most courageous men and women.

1 Who helped Jesus carry the cross on the way to his crucifixion — Simon of Cyrene or Joseph of Arimathea?

2 What did Joseph of Arimathea wrap Jesus' body in — a blanket or a shroud?

3 Who did 'great wonders among the people' — Peter or Stephen?

QUESTION 5

4 A widow once gave the Temple all her money. Were her coins copper or silver?

5 How did four men get their paralyzed friend into a busy house to see Jesus — through the window or the roof?

6 What time of day did Joseph, Mary and baby Jesus flee from King Herod into Egypt — at dawn or at night?

7 Where was Paul when he was put in prison with Silas — Ephesus or Philippi?

QUESTION 9

8 Which book lists heroic people in the Old Testament — Hebrews or Acts?

9 What healed a woman who touched Jesus' robe — her faith or his power?

10 Who was John the Baptist imprisoned for criticising — King Herod or Pontius Pilate?

1 Who was the first Gentile (non-Jew) to be baptized?

2 What is the name for the moment when Jesus appeared to his disciples, speaking to Moses and Elijah?

3 In the Sermon on the Mount, what did Jesus say you should do when someone strikes you on the cheek?

4 Which type of Roman soldier once asked Jesus to heal his paralyzed servant?

5 How did Jesus cure a man who was possessed by demons?

6 What was left behind in the tomb after Jesus had risen?

7 Which word comes before 'Augustus' in the name of the Roman emporer at the time of Jesus' birth?

8 What did John the Baptist say Jesus would baptize people with?

9 What did Jesus say belonged to those who were as innocent as children?

10 What was the meaning of the parable of the Pharisee and the Tax Collector?

These questions are all
about important places.

1 What is the name of the place where Jesus was crucified – Cana or Golgotha?

2 Where was Paul bitten by a viper – Malta or Rome?

3 Where did Peter's mother-in-law live – Emmaus or Capernaum?

4 Where was the Garden of Gethsemane – Mount Sinai or the Mount of Olives?

QUESTION 4

5 On the highway from Jerusalem to Gaza, Philip talked to an official from which country – Egypt or Ethiopia?

6 Jesus once healed a cripple who was lying beside a pool. Where was this pool – Bethsaida or Jericho?

7 Where did Peter cut off someone's ear – Judea or the Garden of Gethsemane?

QUESTION 6

8 On which island was John imprisoned – Patmos or Corsica?

9 Where did Barnabas come from – Cyprus or Rome?

10 Where is the last great battle between good and evil said to happen – Armageddon or Jerusalem?

ANSWERS 1. Golgotha (Matthew 27:33) 2. Malta (Acts 28:1–6) 3. Capernaum (Mark 1:21, 29) 4. The Mount of Olives (Luke 22:39) 5. Ethiopia (Acts 8:27) 6. Bethsaida (John 5:1–18) 7. The Garden of Gethsemane (John 18:10) 8. Patmos (Revelation 1:9) 9. Cyprus (Acts) 10. Armageddon (Revelation 16:16)

Match these sinful people
with their nasty deeds.

1 Salome, daughter of Queen Herodias

A Ordered the death of James

2 Judas Iscariot

B Turned a place of prayer into a 'den of robbers'

3 King Herod Agrippa

C Lied about the price they got for some land

4 Barabbas

D Asked the king for John the Baptist's head

5 Ananias and Sapphira

E Told the guards of Jesus' tomb to lie

6 A priest and a Levite travelling to Jericho

F Betrayed Jesus to his enemies

7 The Jewish elders

G Believed he was not sinful like others

8 A Pharisee, full of the sin of pride

H Ordered the death of Jewish baby boys

9 Money-lenders and traders in the Temple

I Was a murderer

10 King Herod the Great

J Ignored someone in need of help

ANSWERS: 1. D (Matthew 14:6–8) 2. F (Matthew 27:5) 3. A (Acts 12:1–3) 4. I (Luke 23:18–19) 5. C (Acts 5:1–4) 6. J (Luke 10:31–32) 7. E (Matthew 28:11–15) 8. G (Luke 18:11) 9. B (Matthew 21:13) 10. H (Matthew 2:16–18)

Parable Puzzler

Test your knowledge of the stories that Jesus told.

1 In the parable of the talents, where did a man hide one talent — in his house or in the ground?

2 How many bridesmaids didn't have enough lamp oil — five or ten?

3 How many sons did the prodigal son's father have — one or two?

4 To how many servants did the nobleman give money — ten or 100?

5 When asked 'Who is my neighbour?' which parable did Jesus tell — The Good Samaritan or The Prodigal Son?

6 In the parable of the marriage feast, was a man with no wedding clothes welcomed or thrown out?

7 Did a house built on sand fall down or blow away?

8 Was the sower's seed that fell on a path trampled or eaten by birds?

9 What was the mustard seed compared to — Heaven or a temple?

10 Who did the rich man ask for help when he went to Hell — Moses or Abraham?

QUESTION 5

QUESTION 8

ANSWERS 1. In the ground (Matthew 25:14–30) 2. Five (Matthew 25:1–13) 3. Two (Luke 15:11–32) 4. Ten (Luke 19:11–27) 5. The Good Samaritan (Luke 10:29–37) 6. Thrown out (Matthew 22:1–14) 7. It fell down (Matthew 7:24–29) 8. It was eaten by birds (Matthew 13:3–23) 9. Heaven (Matthew 13:31–32) 10. Abraham (Luke 16:19–31)

Helping Hands

Test your knowledge of Jesus' disciples.

1 What was Judas' surname?

2 After Judas betrayed Jesus, who was chosen to replace him – Matthias or Matthew?

3 When Jesus fed the 5000, which disciple told him about the boy with the five loaves and two fish?

4 Which disciple did Jesus call when he was in an office, counting taxes?

5 Which disciple managed to walk a little way on water?

6 How much money did Jesus tell the disciples to take in payment for performing miracles?

7 What did Jesus hear the disciples arguing about one day as they were travelling to Capernaum?

8 The disciples were first called Christians in which city – Athens or Antioch?

9 How many of the disciples had names beginning with 'J'?

10 Which disciple did Jesus see sitting under a fig tree?

Express Yourself

Match these Biblical phrases with their modern interpretations.

 1 "The salt of the earth" (Matthew 5:13)

 2 "To hide one's light under a bushel" (Matthew 5:15)

 3 "A wolf in sheep's clothing" (Matthew 7:15)

 4 "At the eleventh hour" (Matthew 20:1–16)

 5 "A good Samaritan" (Luke 10:30–37)

 A A person who seems harmless but is really dangerous

 B To be modest about your talents

 C People of good character and great value

 D Someone who unselfishly helps a person in need

 E At the last minute

Multiple Choice

Select the correct answer from
the three choices given.

1 Which Pharisee was secretly a follower of Jesus?
a Caiaphas **b** Pontius Pilate **c** Nicodemus

2 Who asked Jesus, 'What is truth?'
a Peter **b** Pontius Pilate **c** a Pharisee

3 How is the day of Jesus' return said to arrive?
a like a fanfare **b** like a storm **c** like a thief in the night

4 Lydia was a wealthy sales lady. What did she sell?
a blue baskets **b** white wool **c** purple cloth

5 According to Paul, what is the root of all kinds of evil?
a desire for fame **b** love of money **c** selfishness

6 Which word refers to Jesus rising from the dead?
a the Resurrection **b** the Ascension **c** the Annunciation

7 Where did Peter raise a woman from the dead?
a Ephesus **b** Rome **c** Lydda

8 Who fell out of a window but was resurrected by Paul?
a Eutychus **b** Lazarus **c** Cornelius

9 Of what is it said New Jerusalem's streets will be made?
a gold **b** diamonds **c** clouds

10 What date did Jesus say he did not know?
a his birth **b** his second coming **c** his death

ANSWERS: 1. c Nicodemus (John 3:1) **2. b** Pontius Pilate (John 18:38) **3. c** Like a thief in the night (1 Thessalonians 5:1–2) **4. c** Purple cloth (Acts 16:13–15) **5. b** Love of money (1 Timothy 6:10) **6. a** The Resurrection **7. c** Lydda (Acts 9:37–43) **8. a** Eutychus (Acts 20:9) **9. a** Gold (Revelation 21:21) **10. b** The date of his second coming (Mark 13:32)

Match each question about
miracles with the right answer.

★ **1** How many gospels tell the
story of the feeding of the
five thousand?

★ **A** One

★ **B** 153

★ **2** At the wedding at Cana, how
many water jars were filled when
Jesus turned water into wine?

★ **C** Four

★ **D** Six

★ **3** When Jesus healed ten lepers,
how many said thank you?

★ **E** Two

★ **4** Jesus healed blind men who cried,
"Have mercy on us, Son of David".
How many blind men were there?

QUESTION 5

★ **5** After Jesus had risen, how many fish
did he help Peter and his friends
catch at the Sea of Tiberias?

Sum It Up

Use the references to look up the numbers and work out these maths problems.

1 Multiply the number of pieces of silver paid to Judas for betraying Jesus by the number of times Peter denied knowing Jesus.

Matthew 26:15, Matthew 26:75

2 Add together the number of times Peter suggested we should forgive someone who wrongs us and the number of times Jesus suggested.

Matthew 18:21–22

3 Multiply the number of disciples that gathered to choose a replacement for Judas by the number of candidates put forward.

Acts 1:15–24

4 Subtract Jesus' age when he began his ministry from the number of 'the beast' in Revelation.

Luke 3:23, Revelation 13:18

5 Add together the number of generations from Abraham to Christ in total, mentioned in the Gospel of Matthew.

Matthew 1:17

1 Elymas was a magician Paul met on the island of Cyprus — true or false?

 2 How long did Paul stay on the island of Malta after he was shipwrecked — one month or three months?

 3 Which New Testament book is a book of prophecy?

 4 Who were known as the 'sons of thunder'?
a Peter and Andrew **b** James and John **c** Paul and Silas

 5 Fill in the missing word: "Blessed are those who have not s _ _ _ and yet believe."

 6 Where did Paul's teaching about Christ result in a riot in support of the goddess, Artemis — Athens or Ephesus?

 7 What 'R' is a city where Paul was placed under house arrest?

 8 **rpolyse** Unscramble the letters to find the name of the disease that Jesus often cured.

 9 Which of the disciples preached to the crowd at Pentecost after Jesus' ascension?

 10 Which book of the New Testament begins with 'G'?

ANSWERS: 1. True (Acts 13:6–12) **2.** Three months (Acts 28:11) **3.** Revelation **4. b** James and John (Mark 3:17) **5.** Seen (John 20:29) **6.** Ephesus (Acts 19:23–41) **7.** Rome (Acts 28:16) **8.** Leprosy (Matthew 8:1–3) **9.** Peter (Acts 2:14) **10.** Galatians.

100 Read and Remember

Read this short story and try to remember as much as you can.

The Last Supper

(Matthew 26:17–35, Mark 14:12–31, Luke 22:7–38, John 13–17)

Jesus and the disciples had entered Jerusalem to celebrate Passover. However, they knew that the Jewish leaders were searching for Jesus, so they could arrest him and have him sentenced to death.

Jesus found a secret room where he and his friends could share the Passover meal in safety. When Thursday came, he sent Peter and John to wait in the city for a man carrying a water jar — he would show them to the room so they could prepare everything.

It was with heavy hearts that Jesus and his friends gathered that night. While the disciples settled at the table, Jesus wrapped a towel around his waist and filled a bowl with water. Then he set about washing the dust from their feet — a job usually done by the lowliest servant. Peter was shocked and tried to stop him, but Jesus insisted. "Follow my example," he explained afterwards. "You must always serve and care for others, as I have just served you."

Then it was time to eat. Jesus took some bread and

asked for God's blessing over it. "This is my body, which will be given for you," he said solemnly. He broke it and shared it out.

Next, Jesus poured a cup of wine and asked for God's blessing over that too. "This is my blood, the sign of a new promise from God. It will be spilled so that everyone's sins will be forgiven," he said. Then he passed the cup around to the disciples.

As the feast got underway, Jesus gave a sorrowful sigh. "One of you will betray me," he said. Cries of protest went up from all around the table, but Jesus said nothing more. Reluctantly, the disciples returned to eating.

Peter murmured to John, who was sitting closest to Jesus, "Ask him who he means."

John spoke into Jesus' ear, and Jesus murmured back, "The one to whom I will give this piece of bread." John and Peter watched as Jesus offered a morsel of bread to Judas Iscariot. "Do what you have to do," he told Judas, "but do it quickly." The disciples all watched in astonishment as Judas left the room without a word.

As the meal drew to a close, Jesus looked around at his dear friends. He announced, "I give you a new commandment; love one another as I have loved you. By showing people love, everyone will know that you are my followers."

"Lord, are you going to leave us?" questioned Peter.

"Yes, I am going away," said Jesus quietly, "and where I am going, you won't be able to follow me — not yet."

"But I will follow you anywhere," cried Peter. "I am ready to die for you!"

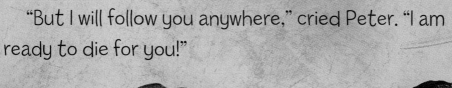

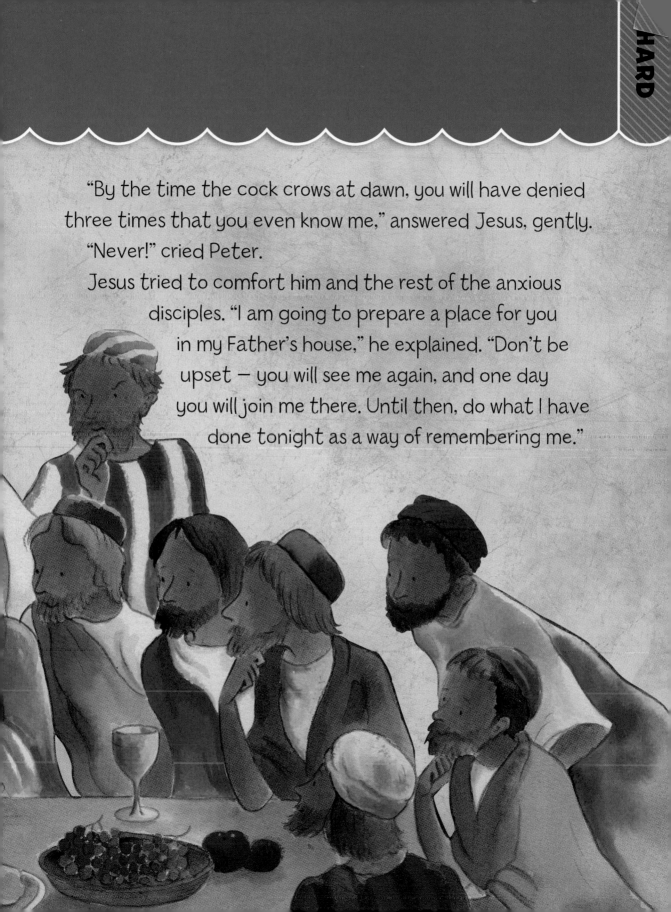

"By the time the cock crows at dawn, you will have denied three times that you even know me," answered Jesus, gently.

"Never!" cried Peter.

Jesus tried to comfort him and the rest of the anxious disciples. "I am going to prepare a place for you in my Father's house," he explained. "Don't be upset — you will see me again, and one day you will join me there. Until then, do what I have done tonight as a way of remembering me."

Now, test your memory on what you have read by answering these questions.

1 What was the name of the festival that Jesus and the disciples were attending in Jerusalem?

2 Why did Jesus find a secret room for the meal?

3 On what day of the week did Jesus have supper with his disciples?

4 How many disciples did Jesus send to prepare the room for the meal?

5 Which disciples did Jesus send?

6 What was the man carrying, who knew where the secret room was?

7 During the Last Supper, what did Jesus say the bread was?

8 What did Jesus say the wine was?

9 Why did Peter try to stop Jesus washing his feet?

10 What new commandment did Jesus give the disciples?

ANSWERS: 1. Passover. 2. The Jewish leaders were searching for Jesus. 3. Thursday. 4. Two. 5. Peter and John. 6. A jar of water. 7. His body. 8. His blood. 9. It was a job usually done by the lowliest servant. 10. Love one another as I have loved you.